Flying Apron's

GLUTEN-FREE & VEGAN BAKING BOOK

Flying Apron's

GLUTEN-FREE & VEGAN BAKING BOOK

JENNIFER KATZINGER

SASQUATCH BOOKS
SEATTLE

Printed in China

Published by Sasquatch Books

Distributed by PGW/Perseus

15 14 13 12 11 10   9 8 7 6 5 4 3 2 1

Cover photographs: Kathryn Barnard

Cover design: Rosebud Eustace

Interior food photographs: Kathryn Barnard

Introduction photographs: Rachelle Longé

Flying Apron Bakery logo (page xv): Elizabeth Dowd

Interior design and composition: Rosebud Eustace

Library of Congress Cataloging-in-Publication Data

Katzinger, Jennifer.

  Flying apron's gluten-free & vegan baking book / Jennifer Katzinger.

     p. cm.

  Includes index.

  ISBN-13: 978-1-57061-629-7

  ISBN-10: 1-57061-629-9

  1. Gluten-free diet—Recipes. 2. Vegan cookery. 3. Baking. I. Title.

  RM237.86.K38 2010

  641.5'638—dc22

                          2009021937

Sasquatch Books

119 South Main Street, Suite 400

Seattle, WA 98104

(206) 467-4300

www.sasquatchbooks.com

custserv@sasquatchbooks.com

For Lillian

Contents

FOREWORD

When I was first diagnosed with celiac disease, I assumed I would never enjoy a baked good again. Vaguely unwell all my life, in the spring of 2005, I suffered a siege of pain and lethargy so intense that many of my closest friends worried I was dying. Finally, a diagnosis gave me a way back to health: celiac disease.

The cure for this condition that had plagued me all my life (and yet I had never heard of it)? Cut out all gluten from my diet. No wheat, rye, barley, triticale, spelt, farro, or contaminated oats, in any form. Ever again.

No problem, at least for me. Having been so sick and sapped of energy, I lost my longing for baguettes and banana cream pie. I focused on fresh foods and finding my health again. I gave away all my baking books and threw away my wooden rolling pin. There would be no pies in my future.

Six weeks later, I wanted a cookie. It's a primal urge, this wish to be comforted with soft crumbs and sweetness. I had been reading recipes for gluten-free cookies, but they were full of flours I had not discovered yet. The only packaged gluten-free cookies available in grocery stores tasted like cardboard dipped in white sugar. Nothing seemed to satisfy my urge.

One Saturday morning, I followed the recommendations of several people online to a spot in the University District in Seattle. Underneath a popular Indian restaurant, next door to a vegan café, a tiny corner space beckoned me. I leaned in the window and saw a commercial mixer whirling away with batter, a wooden table brushed with beige flours, and doughs waiting to be baked. Mostly, I smelled dried dates, cardamom, vanilla, maple syrup, and cinnamon. My memory knew the meaning of this: a bakery. But for the first time since I was diagnosed, I was standing, cash in hand, at a bakery where I could eat.

It was the Flying Apron Bakery.

I babbled to the woman inside about the excitement of knowing I could eat everything before me. She nodded. Later, I realized I had been talking with Jennifer

Katzinger, the brains behind the operation. Lovely and humble, Jennifer has created a business essential to the gluten-free and vegan community in Seattle (and beyond). And she has listened to the people who are grateful for her baked goods, constantly striving to create more options and more memorable tastes. I admire the work she has done, not only in creating Flying Apron Bakery—in all its incarnations (the current airy bakery space in Fremont is about twenty times bigger than that tiny corner bakery was)—but also in writing this book. Jennifer's emphasis on whole grains, cold-pressed oils, and sweeteners other than sugar make these baked goods a boon for people who want healthy treats. So many of you reading will be grateful for these recipes.

I didn't know any of that, then. I just wanted something sweet, without fear that I would grow sick. Before me lay berry corn muffins, loaves of buckwheat bread, ginger pinwheels, and chocolate-covered macaroons. They all looked enticing, and I was stymied by the bounty. But then I saw a large apricot thumbprint cookie. That was it. I reached for it, handed her my money, and turned away smiling. I took one bite and had to stop. A cookie. A warm, delicious cookie, one I never thought I would eat again.

That cookie was such a gift.

—Shauna James Ahern, author of *Gluten-Free Girl*

INTRODUCTION

In the spring of 2002, I opened Flying Apron Bakery with my father, Bill Dowd. In creating our bakery, a few elements were key. We wanted to create treats that were exceptionally nourishing, delicious, unique, and sophisticated. We wanted all of the baked goods to be made with organic ingredients, and it was very important to us that they be made with whole grain flours, alternative sweeteners, and pure cold-pressed oils. Finally, and perhaps most challenging, we wanted the majority of goods to be vegan (made without dairy or eggs) and soy-free (since soy is a major allergen).

We chose to go vegan because such focus on a plant-based diet would greatly reduce our carbon footprint. And we wanted to make baked goods that as many people could eat as possible, despite ailments and food allergies. Customers appreciate what we offer for various reasons: many are allergic to dairy and eggs; others prefer a vegan bakery because they are concerned for animal welfare; and some are neither allergic nor vegan but are simply very health-conscious and careful about what they consume.

When Flying Apron Bakery first opened, we were almost entirely vegan (we used to offer two cookies that used eggs and dairy; today, we are 100 percent egg- and dairy-free), offering wholesome, wheat-free, and alternatively sweetened foods. We used flours such as spelt, barley, and oat, along with brown rice flour, quinoa flour, garbanzo bean flour, corn flour, and cornmeal. That most of our baked goods were made with gluten-free grains was pure coincidence. At the time, I didn't know that gluten-free foods mattered to so many, but as our customers began asking if our foods were gluten-free, I decided to add more gluten-free offerings to our menu. I began playing with more gluten-free ingredients, experimenting and taking notes until I achieved wonderfully tasty results.

Running Flying Apron Bakery has in some ways been an emotional roller coaster. I have met so many people affected by gluten intolerance and heard so many stories about the different ways their symptoms manifested. My heart went out to the kids I met who couldn't have birthday cake or pizza at a friend's party, and to the adults I met who broke down in tears because they hadn't been to a bakery in years where they would actually be able to eat anything on the shelves. Their stories, and my successful

gluten-free experiments, led me to shift the bakery to be completely gluten-free. The immense gratitude that customers have since expressed has been surprising and deeply moving. I couldn't have predicted that Flying Apron Bakery would touch so many people so profoundly—and all by way of simple baked goods.

My father and I began Flying Apron together with all the creative and physical energy we had (and that was all we had!). The bakery's first home was located in Seattle's University District: we started small, with a space about as big as a walk-in closet. Although he has since moved on to other ventures, my father made it possible for me to go down this road by taking the first steps with me. He facilitated a growth in me that, although difficult at times, I am most grateful for.

Over the last seven years, Flying Apron Bakery has evolved while maintaining the core of its essence. In the bakery's first humble location, we had a charming take-out window and we began our wholesale business. Many of our first customers became special friends, and I have such fond memories of the thrill of those first two

years, despite the grueling hours of working day and night. One of my first customers is now my husband—on our first date he helped me deliver the very first wedding cake I ever made! Our own wedding took place many baked goods later.

As the wholesale business grew and our small physical space did not, I knew we had to find another wholesale kitchen. In the summer of 2004, we took our next big step, moving to a larger space underneath the Elliott Bay Book Company in downtown Seattle's historic Pioneer Square. This was an exciting time and a lesson in learning how to oversee two locations while trusting others to do the baking.

In 2006, Flying Apron began its next pursuit: participating in farmers markets. Being a part of our local farmers markets has been so fulfilling. The community setting, the ritual, the vibrant colors of all the fresh produce, the relationships I've made with customers and neighboring vendors—it's one of the richest experiences I've ever had. Being a part of the local farmers market means engaging in something timeless and connected to the cycle of life. Customers' enthusiasm at our local farmers markets gave me the courage to take the next step with the bakery, and that is how we arrived at our current location in the Fremont district of Seattle.

The Fremont location is now where we do it all. We left both the University District and Pioneer Square locations in 2007, and we at last have the space for customers to come and enjoy our vibrant pastries and savory fare in a bakery café. And the kitchen is large enough to do all of our wholesale and farmers market baking, too.

It's hard to find words to express the pure excitement and gratitude that I feel daily at Flying Apron Bakery. Mostly, I am grateful for the beautiful and talented

people who make the bakery's wheels turn. Their dedication, patience, and positive regard have truly enriched
my life. I am amazed that in a small business that still
has to focus on profit margins, cash flow, and efficiency,
our relationships and interactions are so authentic, joy-
ful, and respectful.

flying apron bakery

As the bakery has developed and grown over the
years, so has our awareness about the benefits of unrefined flours and sweeteners, pure oils, organic ingredients,
and relying more heavily on plant-based foods. Simultaneously, there is a growing
awareness of food sensitivities, allergies, and celiac disease. According to an article
published September 15, 2007, in the *British Medical Journal*, for each person diagnosed with celiac disease, eight cases go undetected. It is estimated that in the United
States alone, there are 2.67 million people living with celiac disease who have yet to
be diagnosed.

The increasing need for dietary lifestyle changes makes this feel like the right
time to share Flying Apron's recipes. I would like to reach beyond our bakery's
location to help more people transition with ease to a gluten-free and vegan diet. My
hope is that these recipes will benefit the home cook in many ways. Whether you
wish to avoid cholesterol; benefit from the goodness of whole foods; utilize wholesome sweeteners; add variety to your diet; bake and cook without gluten, dairy, eggs,
or soy; or simply add joy to your life and the lives of those you love through delicious
foods, I hope these recipes delight and inspire you. Bon appétit!

Flying Apron's

GLUTEN-FREE & VEGAN BAKING BOOK

Chapter 1

ABOUT THE RECIPES

If you are accustomed to other vegan or gluten-free cookbooks, you will notice that the recipes in this book probably look quite different than what you are used to. There are many characteristics that make these recipes unique.

Soy-Free, Dairy-Free, and Egg-Free

All of the recipes I've included in this book reflect what we make at the bakery—they are gluten-free, plant-based, and made from whole foods. So that they can be enjoyed by all, the recipes are also very allergy friendly: they are soy-free, dairy-free, and egg-free—a rare combination.

I've noticed over the years that many vegan cookbooks depend heavily on soy as a substitute for eggs and milk. While soy is a wonderfully nutritious food, there are many people who suffer from soy allergies, so its use is omitted here. Aside from being less allergenic, soy-, dairy-, and egg-free foods have the added bonus of being cholesterol-free.

Whole Grains and Organic

Many gluten-free recipes rely heavily on refined flours and starches, such as tapioca starch, potato starch, eggs, egg replacement products, and white rice flour. You will notice that the flours used in these recipes are all made with whole grains. Given the health benefits of whole grains, at Flying Apron we strongly prefer their use over processed and refined flours and starches. In addition, the oils suggested in this cookbook are pure, organic, and cold pressed, and the majority are low in saturated fats.

The sweeteners used in many cookbooks tend to be refined and unhealthy. Instead of those, the recipes that follow utilize natural sweeteners such as maple syrup, agave syrup, fruit juice, stevia, and organic whole cane sugar.

Finally, note that none of the recipes call specifically for organic ingredients. That said, I do enthusiastically encourage you to choose organic ingredients whenever possible. When you choose organic ingredients you are selecting ingredients free from harmful pesticides as well as pulled from a richer soil, which in turn provides more minerals and nutrients for our bodies. You are supporting sustainable farming methods that protect and enhance the microorganisms and biodiversity of the soil and the surrounding ecosystems. And the farmhands working on organic farms are safe from exposure to the carcinogenic pesticides so abundantly used on nonorganic farms. At Flying Apron Bakery, we have made this commitment to organics, and our customers have embraced our decision, telling us that they feel all the more healthy for eating this way.

Buy Local

Recently, I have been greatly influenced by author Michael Pollan (*The Omnivore's Dilemma, In Defense of Food*), who emphasizes the importance of getting as many ingredients locally as possible. Finding out which local ingredients here in the Pacific Northwest are gluten-free has been a fascinating process. I've been excited to discover such wonderful regional ingredients as chestnut flour, hazelnut flour, corn flour and cornmeal, amaranth flour, honey, and oil made from the grape seeds of some nearby wineries. Of course, "local" ingredients vary from one locality to another; I encourage you to modify these recipes to adapt to what local options are available to you.

Gluten-Free Baking versus Traditional Baking

Cooks and bakers accustomed to traditional baking may find gluten-free baking much different than what they are used to. If you are new to gluten-free baking, I strongly advise you to read through and study an entire recipe before starting, and to take care when shaping baked goods and checking for doneness. This may take some experimentation, but with a little bit of practice you will gain familiarity with how the doughs should feel. Please also be sure to read through all chapter introductions, as a number contain helpful techniques that really make a difference. You will find notes pertaining to successful scone-making, special instructions that apply to all of the bread recipes in this cookbook, and tips on assembly and baking in the chapters for pies and cakes.

Staple Ingredients to Have on Hand

You will notice I tend to rely on the same basic ingredients in many recipes. Helpful ingredients to keep in your cupboard are:

brown rice flour
garbanzo bean flour
buckwheat flour
teff flour
quinoa flour
corn flour
cornmeal
fava bean flour
chestnut flour
hazelnut flour
gluten-free oats

almonds
walnuts
pecans
flax meal
canola oil
extra-virgin cold-pressed
    olive oil
coconut oil or palm oil
maple syrup, agave
    syrup, or concentrated
    fruit juice

organic whole cane sugar
brown rice syrup
rice milk
baking soda
baking powder
active dry yeast
sea salt
xanthan gum
arrowroot powder
pure vanilla

If you have celiac disease or are gluten-intolerant, it's a good idea to continuously check that the sources of your ingredients are safe from gluten contamination. There are some trustworthy brands such as Bob's Red Mill and Lundberg, for example. Some companies that sell brown rice flour, bean flours, oats, or other would-be gluten-free ingredients mill where other gluten grains are milled, making what should be a gluten-free ingredient a carrier of gluten. Thankfully, awareness of gluten intolerance has grown so tremendously that buying gluten-free ingredients has become increasingly easier over the years. Check with the Gluten Intolerance Group (www.gluten.net) for sources of gluten-free ingredients near you.

Many of the recipes in this book give you a variety of sweeteners from which to choose. For many new to sugar alternatives, these sweeteners may be unfamiliar. When making your choice, know that agave syrup is the least sweet option, maple syrup will create a robust and perhaps slightly heavier texture (which I personally love), and concentrated fruit juices are significantly sweeter than the agave and will achieve a lighter texture than the maple syrup.

With regard to concentrated fruit juices, I recommend Aunt Patty's concentrated pear juice and Mystic Lake Dairy's pineapple-peach-pear juice concentrate (see Resources). Both of these pour like a rich golden syrup. Many concentrated fruit juices can also be purchased frozen. Make sure to cook down the frozen juice until a syrupy consistency is reached. You can then store any extra reduced concentrate in the refrigerator.

All sweeteners are set in **boldface** within recipe ingredient lists to help you easily pinpoint them and determine if the recipe is right for you. Many of the headnotes offer suggestions for using an alternate sweetener when applicable as well. Do experiment with your sweetener of choice until you get the outcome you like best.

Many of this book's recipes call for canola oil. You may find this surprising; for the first two years of the bakery, we baked with only organic extra-virgin cold-pressed olive oil. I find the taste of olive oil in baked goods to be the ultimate, but as time went on, we realized the price of olive oil was something to be reckoned with, so we switched to organic safflower oil. Recently, after studying the works of Dr. Dean Ornish—best known for his plant-based diets that have repeatedly shown to be successful in reversing cardiovascular diseases—we found that organic canola oil could be a healthier alternative. A bonus: I soon found that the taste of canola oil was more complementary and subtle than safflower oil in baking. Feel free, though, to substitute your own favorite oil for the canola oil called for in the recipes; you will still have fantastic results.

A Brief Overview of Wheat Intolerance, Gluten Intolerance, and Celiac Disease

For those readers who are new to wheat and gluten intolerances and celiac disease, it may be helpful to understand their differences. Please note, though, that this is just a brief overview for informative purposes. Please consult with your health practitioner for detailed answers to any questions you may have.

Doctors believe that people can develop **wheat** or **gluten intolerances** for a number of reasons, even from simply eating too much wheat or gluten over a long period of time. From the first day Flying Apron opened, my customers have shared with me their struggles with wheat and gluten intolerance, and I have been surprised at the variety of their symptoms—each case is unique. The good news is that while intolerances are incredibly uncomfortable and mystifying until identified (often by an elimination diet or a blood test), in many cases they can be overcome by avoiding the food and giving the body adequate time to heal.

Many believe that our wheat sensitivities began when we started hybridizing and genetically modifying wheat and growing predominately hard winter wheat with the highest protein content (and therefore the highest gluten content). As an informed consumer, I can share one truth that predominates: there are great benefits to enjoying a well-rounded variety of plant foods without relying heavily on one food excessively. So when cooking and baking for friends and family members who have no food sensitivities, you can celebrate that they too will at the very least benefit from the added variety of ingredients that you will supply in their diet and life.

Celiac disease, on the other hand, is an autoimmune disease and not an allergy or food sensitivity. Generally speaking, the disease severely damages the digestive tract so that when the smallest amount of gluten enters a person's body, that person will create antibodies that attack his or her own stomach's lining. As a result, the bumps and valleys in the digestive tract that normally help absorb nutrients from foods become flattened and smooth and unable to absorb nutrients. The symptoms and consequences can be devastating. Someone with celiac disease must avoid gluten for the rest of his or her life, and always be careful not to ingest any food that might have gluten contamination.

A Final Note

Developing these recipes has been a joy. Creating something that nourishes others has been such a fulfilling experience for me over the years. I wish you great pleasure and health as you dive into a new way of nurturing your taste buds and your loved ones, and I hope this cookbook encourages you to experiment with many new ingredients!

Chapter 2

MORNING PASTRIES

A delicious and nourishing morning pastry is such a celebratory way to greet any day. The selection of scones, muffins, and coffee cakes that follow offer a variety of flavors and richness. You will find that most of them are sweetened with maple syrup, fruit juice, or agave syrup. The tea cakes and coffee cakes also make for a very gratifying finish to any meal. I often serve the Honey Cornmeal Cake (page 31) with fresh peaches for dessert during the summer months, and the Almond Cake (page 35) is dressy enough to serve as an evening finale.

Scones

Currant Zest Scones
Blueberry Cinnamon Scones
Oaty Flying Apron Biscuits
Buckwheat Flying Apron Biscuits
Berry Tea Biscuits
Apricot Almond Individuals

Muffins

Maple Berry Muffins
Berry Corn Muffins
Dark Chocolate Muffins
Matcha Muffins
Lemon Poppy Seed Muffins
Carrot Muffins

Coffee Cakes, Tea Breads, and Bars

Earl Grey Tea Cake
Honey Cornmeal Cake
Berry Oat Wondie Bars
Pumpkin Glory Loaf
Almond Cake

Scones

Many of the scone recipes here call for chilling the dough for at least three hours (with the exception of the Apricot Almond Individuals on page 20). Because scones are often enjoyed for breakfast, I recommend making your dough the night before and storing it in a sealed container in the refrigerator until the next morning. That way, when you wake up, you can simply form your scones and pop them in the oven for a timely hot breakfast. All scone doughs can be refrigerated for up to four days and frozen for up to one month.

Currant Zest Scones

These scones are perfect with a cup of English breakfast tea. When I visit my sister in York, England, we often indulge in what is known as a "Fat Rascal" scone. The citrus zest and currants in this scone remind me of the Fat Rascal, and with one bite I am transported to sweet memories of time spent in the cold north of England.

8 SCONES

    2¾ cups brown rice flour

    1½ cups plus 1 tablespoon garbanzo bean flour

    1 teaspoon baking powder

    ½ teaspoon baking soda

    ¾ teaspoon sea salt

    ½ teaspoon orange zest

    1 cup canola oil

    1 cup **organic whole cane sugar**

    1 cup rice milk

    ¾ cup currants

1. Combine the brown rice flour, garbanzo bean flour, baking powder, baking soda, salt, and orange zest in a large bowl. In the bowl of a standing mixer fitted with the paddle attachment, combine the canola oil and organic whole cane sugar until well mixed. With the mixer on low speed, add the flour mixture and rice milk alternately, a little at a time, until well mixed, about 3 minutes. Chill the dough for at least 3 hours or overnight.

2. Preheat the oven to 360 degrees F.

3. Dust your counter liberally with brown rice flour. Knead the currants into the chilled dough and pat the dough into a 2-inch-thick disc. Cut the disc into 8 wedges. Place the wedges onto a greased or parchment-lined baking sheet, spaced evenly apart. Bake until scones are golden brown and firm to the touch, about 30 minutes.

Blueberry Cinnamon Scones

Blueberries and cinnamon are like good friends—they should be together as often as possible. Here, you will find the combination quite satisfying.

8 SCONES

2¾ cups brown rice flour

1½ cups plus 1 tablespoon garbanzo bean flour

1 teaspoon baking powder

½ teaspoon baking soda

¾ teaspoon sea salt

1 teaspoon ground cinnamon

1 cup canola oil

1 cup **organic whole cane sugar**

1 cup rice milk

¾ cup frozen blueberries

1. Combine the brown rice flour, garbanzo bean flour, baking powder, baking soda, salt, and cinnamon in a large bowl. In the bowl of a standing mixer fitted with the paddle attachment, combine the canola oil and organic whole cane sugar until well mixed. With the mixer on low speed, add the flour mixture and rice milk alternately, a little at a time, until well mixed, about 3 minutes. Chill the dough for at least 3 hours or overnight.

2. Preheat the oven to 375 degrees F.

3. Dust your counter liberally with brown rice flour. Knead the blueberries into the chilled dough and pat the dough into a 2-inch-thick disc. Cut the disc into 8 wedges. Place the wedges onto a greased or parchment-lined baking sheet, spaced evenly apart. Bake until scones are golden brown and firm to the touch, about 30 minutes.

Oaty Flying Apron Biscuits

Grinding oats to make oat flour is a bit time consuming, but these biscuits are well worth the effort. If you are not a raspberry fan, feel free to substitute any kind of fruit you like. Raisins and nuts are also great additions. These are even great plain.

12 TO 15 BISCUITS

> 5¼ cups gluten-free oats
>
> 1½ cups teff flour
>
> 2½ teaspoons baking powder
>
> ¾ teaspoon sea salt
>
> 1 cup canola oil or extra-virgin olive oil
>
> 1 cup **organic whole cane sugar**
>
> ½ cup rice milk
>
> 1 cup raspberries

1. Run 4 cups of the oats through a home flour mill or Vita-Mix blender until pulverized. (Alternatively, you can run the oats through a food processor, but because the resulting oat flour will not be as fine, you will need to chill the dough for at least 6 hours to achieve a sturdier dough that will not spread in the oven.)

2. Combine the oat flour, the remaining 1¼ cups oats, and the teff flour, baking powder, and salt in a large bowl. In the bowl of a standing mixer fitted with the paddle attachment, combine the canola oil and organic whole cane sugar until well mixed. With the mixer on low speed, add the flour mixture and rice milk alternately, a little at a time, until well mixed, about 3 minutes. Chill the dough for at least 3 hours or overnight.

3. Preheat the oven to 375 degrees F.

4. Dust your counter liberally with brown rice flour. Gently mix the raspberries into the dough with your hands, being careful not to break them. Roll the chilled dough into a 1½-inch-thick disc and cut into biscuits using your favorite 3- to 4-inch cookie or biscuit cutter. Place the biscuits onto a greased or parchment-lined baking sheet, spaced 2 inches apart. For a more rustic biscuit, you can also drop 3-inch scoops of dough directly onto the prepared baking sheet.

5. Bake until biscuits are golden brown and firm to the touch, 15 to 20 minutes.

Buckwheat Flying Apron Biscuits

These are delightful plain and quite cute dusted with powdered organic whole cane sugar when they come out of the oven. Some delicious optional additions are berries, chopped nuts, or raisins.

15 TO 20 BISCUITS

> 1¼ cups buckwheat flour
>
> 3¼ cups brown rice flour
>
> 2½ teaspoons baking powder
>
> ¾ teaspoon sea salt
>
> 1 cup canola oil or extra-virgin olive oil
>
> 1 cup **organic whole cane sugar**
>
> ¾ cup rice milk

1. Combine the buckwheat flour, brown rice flour, baking powder, and salt in a large bowl. In the bowl of a standing mixer fitted with the paddle attachment, combine the canola oil and organic whole cane sugar until well mixed. With the mixer on low speed, add the flour mixture and rice milk alternately, a little at a time, until well mixed, about 3 minutes. Chill the dough for at least 3 hours or overnight.

2. Preheat the oven to 375 degrees F.

3. Dust your counter liberally with brown rice flour. Roll the chilled dough into a 1-inch-thick disc and cut into biscuits using your favorite 3-inch cookie or biscuit cutter. Place the biscuits onto a greased or parchment-lined baking sheet, spaced 1 inch apart. Bake until golden brown and firm to the touch, 15 to 20 minutes.

4. For a more rustic biscuit, you can also drop 2- to 3-inch scoops of dough directly onto a prepared baking sheet. If you choose to make these free-form biscuits, there's no need to chill the dough; just preheat the oven to 375 degrees F and bake until golden brown and firm to the touch, about 15 minutes.

Berry Tea Biscuits

I included berry tea biscuits in this section as they have ingredients very similar to the ones in the scones. However, the absence of cinnamon, the berries placed just on top, and the circular flattened shape create a slightly different texture and flavor. Personally, I love to bake these with big, juicy strawberries or marionberries.

12 TO 15 BISCUITS

2¾ cups brown rice flour

1½ cups plus 1 tablespoon garbanzo bean flour

1 teaspoon baking powder

½ teaspoon baking soda

¾ teaspoon sea salt

1 cup canola oil

1 cup **organic whole cane sugar**

1 cup rice milk

1 cup berries

Turbinado sugar, for sprinkling on top of the biscuits

1. Combine the brown rice flour, garbanzo bean flour, baking powder, baking soda, and salt in a large bowl. In the bowl of a standing mixer fitted with the paddle attachment, combine the canola oil and organic whole cane sugar until well mixed. With the mixer on low speed, add the flour mixture and rice milk alternately, a little at a time, until well mixed, about 3 minutes. Chill the dough for at least 3 hours or overnight.

2. Preheat the oven to 360 degrees F.

3. Place baseball-sized balls of dough onto a greased or parchment-lined baking sheet, spaced 2 inches apart. Lightly flatten the balls with the palm of your hand.

4. Place 4 berries on top of each disc of dough, pressing them in gently. Sprinkle turbinado sugar on top. Bake until golden and firm to the touch, about 30 minutes.

Apricot Almond Individuals

If you are an apricot lover, you have to try these biscuits. This is one of the first Flying Apron Bakery recipes I developed. This is a very versatile treat as it can be enjoyed for breakfast or as a satisfying midday snack. The apricot almond individuals can be made into miniatures for a festive tea party too. You will just want to shorten your baking time accordingly.

8 TO 12 BISCUITS

> 2 cups teff flour
>
> 1 teaspoon baking powder
>
> ½ cup extra-virgin olive oil
>
> ½ cup **organic whole cane sugar**
>
> 1 cup Apricot Puree (page 49)
>
> 1 teaspoon almond extract
>
> 18 dried apricots, halved
>
> 36 whole almonds
>
> **Turbinado sugar**, for sprinkling on top of the biscuits

1. Preheat the oven to 360 degrees F.

2. Combine the teff flour and baking powder in a medium-size bowl. In the bowl of a standing mixer fitted with the paddle attachment, combine the olive oil, organic whole cane sugar, apricot puree, and almond extract until well mixed. With the mixer on low speed, add the flour mixture a little at a time until well mixed, about 3 minutes.

3. Place baseball-sized balls of dough onto a greased or parchment-lined baking sheet, spaced 2 inches apart. Lightly flatten the balls with the palm of your hand. Arrange 3 apricot halves and 3 whole almonds on top of each biscuit. Sprinkle turbinado sugar on top.

4. Bake until the biscuits are firm and golden brown, 20 to 25 minutes, rotating the pan halfway through baking.

Muffins

I find that the perfect muffin is moist; subtly sweet; has a slightly firm, browned top; and contains surprise bursts of fruit flavor or texture with bits of nuts interspersed. At the bakery the muffin pan we use is 3 inches in diameter, which makes quite a large muffin. A smaller muffin tin will also work marvelously. When using a smaller muffin pan, you will need to adjust your baking time by decreasing it incrementally. For a 2-inch muffin, for example, bake your muffins 5 to 10 minutes less.

Maple Berry Muffins

These muffins are so satisfying, moist, and tender. This recipe originated when a customer came to me for a vanilla cake but was opposed to having the cake sweetened with fruit juices due to allergies. She suggested I use maple syrup instead. The result was gorgeous. A very talented baker at Flying Apron (at the time), Ailee Regal, had the ingenious idea to use this new maple-sweetened version of the cake batter for maple pecan muffins. These muffins have been a hit. If you prefer, you can replace the berries with ½ cup of chopped pecans to make Maple Pecan Muffins.

12 MUFFINS

> 1½ cups brown rice flour
>
> ¾ cup garbanzo bean flour, sifted
>
> 1½ teaspoons baking soda
>
> ¾ teaspoon sea salt
>
> ½ teaspoon ground cinnamon
>
> ½ cup extra-virgin olive oil or canola oil
>
> 1 cup water
>
> ½ teaspoon apple cider vinegar
>
> 1½ teaspoons vanilla extract
>
> 1 cup **maple syrup**
>
> ½ cup raspberries
>
> ½ cup blueberries

1. Preheat the oven to 375 degrees F.

2. Combine the brown rice flour, garbanzo bean flour, baking soda, salt, and cinnamon in a large bowl. In the bowl of a standing mixer fitted with the whisk attachment, combine the olive oil, water, apple cider vinegar, vanilla, and maple syrup. With the mixer on low speed, slowly add the flour mixture to the olive oil mixture until smooth.

3. Divide the batter evenly among 8 muffin tin cups lined with paper liners. Drop the berries on top and bake until muffin tops are golden and slightly firm to the touch, 20 to 25 minutes.

Berry Corn Muffins

Years ago, a gluten-intolerant little girl asked me to give a baking lesson at her birthday party. This berry corn muffin was one of the recipes I developed specifically for her celebration. The children were excellent little bakers and were able to make these muffins beautifully from start to finish. I love the contrasting color of the yellow cornmeal against the blueberries. And the touch of lemon really ties all the flavors together perfectly.

12 MUFFINS

¾ cup brown rice flour

⅓ cup cornmeal

¼ cup corn flour

¾ teaspoon baking soda

¾ teaspoon sea salt

½ cup canola oil

¾ cup **organic whole cane sugar**

1 cup plus 3 tablespoons water

1 teaspoon vanilla extract

1 tablespoon flax meal

½ teaspoon lemon oil

½ cup blueberries

½ cup raspberries

1. Preheat the oven to 375 degrees F.

2. Combine the brown rice flour, cornmeal, corn flour, baking soda, and salt in a large bowl. In the bowl of a standing mixer fitted with the whisk attachment, combine the canola oil, organic whole cane sugar, water, vanilla, flax meal, and lemon oil until well mixed. With the mixer on low speed, slowly add the flour mixture until smooth.

3. Divide the batter evenly among 8 lined or greased muffin tin cups; batter should stop ¼ inch from the top of each cup. Drop the berries on top and bake until muffin tops are golden and slightly firm to the touch, 20 to 25 minutes.

Dark Chocolate Muffins

Usually I would say chocolate in the morning is probably too rich. However, these are maple syrup–sweetened (and not overly sweet). Also, the boost of cocoa powder gives me an extra spring to my step, which I sometimes appreciate on an early morning.

18 MUFFINS

¾ cup sifted garbanzo bean or chestnut flour

1⅓ cups sifted cocoa powder

1¾ cups brown rice flour

1½ teaspoons sea salt

1 tablespoon baking soda

1 cup canola oil

2 cups water

2 cups **maple syrup**

1 cup raspberries (optional)

¾ cup chopped nuts (optional)

½ cup chopped dairy-free dark chocolate (optional)

1. Preheat the oven to 375 degrees F.

2. Combine the garbanzo bean flour, cocoa powder, brown rice flour, salt, and baking soda in a large bowl. In the bowl of a standing mixer fitted with the whisk attachment, combine the canola oil, water, and maple syrup. With the mixer on low speed, slowly add the flour mixture to the canola oil mixture until smooth.

3. Working quickly to get the most out of the rising agent, divide the batter evenly among 14 lined or greased muffin tin cups. Drop raspberries, nuts, and/or dark chocolate on top. Bake until tops are firm to the touch and a toothpick inserted into the muffin comes out clean, about 25 minutes.

Matcha Muffins

A muffin for the super health zealot! Matcha is a powdered Japanese green tea that is extraordinary for its nutty taste and health properties (even more so than regular green tea). The agave sweetener in this muffin is very subtle; in fact, these muffins may not be sweet enough for some. For those seeking a sweeter muffin, I recommend replacing the agave with maple syrup or concentrated fruit juice. These muffins also work well with the addition of fruit (1 cup of your favorite berries is a great choice); and if the coconut is too rich for your liking, you may omit it.

12 MUFFINS

> 1½ cups brown rice flour
>
> ¾ cup garbanzo bean flour, sifted
>
> 1½ teaspoons baking soda
>
> ¾ teaspoon sea salt
>
> 2½ teaspoons matcha
>
> ½ cup extra-virgin olive oil or canola oil
>
> 1 cup water
>
> ½ teaspoon apple cider vinegar
>
> 1½ teaspoons vanilla extract
>
> 1 cup **agave syrup**
>
> ½ teaspoon lemon oil
>
> ½ cup shredded toasted coconut

1. Preheat the oven to 375 degrees F.

2. Combine the brown rice flour, garbanzo bean flour, baking soda, salt, and matcha in a large bowl. In the bowl of a standing mixer fitted with the whisk attachment, combine the olive oil, water, apple cider vinegar, vanilla, agave syrup, and lemon oil. With the mixer on low speed, slowly add the flour mixture to the olive oil mixture until thoroughly combined. Mix in the coconut.

3. Divide the batter evenly among 10 muffin tin cups lined with paper liners. Bake until muffin tops are golden and firm to the touch, 20 to 25 minutes.

Lemon Poppy Seed Muffins

Lemon and poppy seeds are a classic combination for a reason! When deciding on a sweetener, keep in mind that concentrated fruit juice will create a sweeter result than agave syrup, and maple syrup will lend a richer, full-bodied flavor equal in sweetness to the fruit juice. Choose accordingly, depending on your preference.

12 MUFFINS

    1½ cups brown rice flour

    ¾ cup garbanzo bean flour

    1½ teaspoons baking soda

    ¾ teaspoon sea salt

    ½ cup canola oil

    1 cup water

    ½ teaspoon apple cider vinegar

    1½ teaspoons vanilla extract

    1 cup **agave syrup**, **maple syrup**, or **concentrated pear juice**

    ½ teaspoon lemon oil

    ⅓ cup poppy seeds

1. Preheat the oven to 375 degrees F.

2. Combine the brown rice flour, garbanzo bean flour, baking soda, and salt in a large bowl. In the bowl of a standing mixer fitted with the whisk attachment, combine the canola oil, water, apple cider vinegar, vanilla, agave syrup, and lemon oil. With the mixer on low speed, slowly add the flour mixture to the canola oil mixture until thoroughly combined. Mix in the poppy seeds.

3. Divide the batter evenly among 9 lined or greased muffin tin cups. Bake until muffin tops are golden and firm to the touch, 20 to 25 minutes.

Carrot Muffins

This is a hearty, high-fiber muffin that you'll feel good about indulging in. The burst of sweetness from the raisins, the moistness of the carrots, the crunch of the walnuts, and the texture and nuttiness from the coconut meet my every sensory need in a muffin!

18 MUFFINS

   2 cups brown rice flour

   1¼ cups garbanzo bean flour

   1½ teaspoons baking soda

   ¾ teaspoon sea salt

   1½ teaspoons ground cinnamon

   1 cup canola oil

   2 cups water

   1 tablespoon vanilla extract

   2 cups **agave syrup** or **concentrated fruit juice** (I recommend Mystic Lake Dairy's pineapple-peach-pear concentrate)

   1¼ cups grated carrots (about 5 medium carrots)

   2½ cups shredded unsweetened coconut

   2 cups chopped walnuts or pecans

   1 cup golden raisins

1. Preheat the oven to 350 degrees F.

2. Combine the brown rice flour, garbanzo bean flour, baking soda, salt, and cinnamon in a large bowl. In a second large bowl, combine the canola oil, water, vanilla, and agave syrup. In a third large bowl, combine the carrots, coconut, walnuts, and raisins. Slowly whisk the flour mixture into the canola oil mixture until thoroughly combined. Gently fold in the carrot mixture until just combined.

3. Divide the batter evenly among 15 lined or greased muffin tin cups. Bake until muffin tops are golden and firm to the touch, 20 to 25 minutes.

Coffee Cakes, Tea Breads, and Bars

Coffee cakes, tea breads, and bars stand out to me as especially wonderful baked goods as they often serve the delicious purpose of being offered as sweet homemade gifts. Also, brunches and tea parties are rarely held in their absence! Even while being informal treats, they certainly make their impact on our kitchen tables.

Earl Grey Tea Cake

This cake is my everything. I love it for breakfast or for a light dessert. It's also perfect for an afternoon tea party.

TWO 8½- BY 4½-INCH LOAVES, OR ONE 10-INCH SQUARE CAKE

> 4 cups brown rice flour
>
> 2 cups garbanzo bean flour
>
> 1 tablespoon baking soda
>
> 1 teaspoon sea salt
>
> 1⅓ cups canola oil
>
> 3 cups brewed Earl Grey tea
>
> 1 tablespoon plus 1 teaspoon vanilla extract
>
> 3 cups **maple syrup**
>
> ¾ cup currants

1. Preheat the oven to 375 degrees F.

2. Combine the brown rice flour, garbanzo bean flour, baking soda, and salt in a large bowl. In a separate large bowl, combine the canola oil, tea, vanilla, and maple syrup. Slowly whisk the flour mixture into the canola oil mixture until thoroughly combined. Mix in the currants.

3. Line the bottoms of two 8½- by 4½-inch loaf pans or one 10-inch square cake pan with parchment paper. Pour in the batter and bake until the cake springs back when you press the center with your finger, 45 minutes to 1 hour. After the cake has cooled, run a knife along the inside of the pan to aid in turning the cake out for serving.

Honey Cornmeal Cake

A play on an Italian classic. The combination of olive oil and honey makes me swoon. I particularly like chestnut honey in this recipe. Serve this cake with fresh peaches in the summer.

ONE 9-INCH CAKE

> 1¾ cups brown rice flour
>
> ¼ cup cornmeal
>
> ¼ cup corn flour
>
> 1½ teaspoons baking soda
>
> ¾ teaspoon sea salt
>
> ½ cup extra-virgin olive oil
>
> 1 cup **honey**
>
> 1½ teaspoons vanilla extract
>
> Zest of 1 medium lemon, approximately 2 teaspoons
>
> ¼ cup flax meal
>
> 1 cup rice milk
>
> ½ cup blueberries, ½ cup blackberries, or 2 peaches, sliced (optional)
>
> **Organic whole cane sugar**, for sprinkling on top of the cake (optional)

1. Preheat the oven to 375 degrees F.

2. Combine the brown rice flour, cornmeal, corn flour, baking soda, and salt in a large bowl. In the bowl of a standing mixer fitted with the paddle attachment, combine the olive oil, honey, vanilla, lemon zest, and flax meal until well mixed. With the mixer on low speed, add the flour mixture and rice milk alternately, a little at a time, until well mixed, about 3 minutes.

3. Line the bottom of a 9-inch round cake pan with parchment paper, or grease and dust with brown rice flour. Pour in the batter. Decorate with the berries or peach slices and sprinkle with the organic whole cane sugar. Bake until the cake springs back when you press the center with your finger, about 50 minutes.

Berry Oat Wondie Bars

A favorite among many of my customers, family, and friends. The cobblerlike topping over a thick layer of berries is hard to resist. These won't last long in the house! Our favorite berry combination at Flying Apron is raspberries and blueberries.

12 BARS

> 5 cups gluten-free oats, divided
>
> ¼ cup **brown rice syrup**
>
> ½ cup **maple syrup**, divided
>
> 1 cup extra-virgin olive oil
>
> ½ teaspoon salt
>
> 1 teaspoon vanilla extract
>
> 3½ cups mixed berries
>
> ¼ cup corn flour or arrowroot powder

1. Place 2 cups of the oats in a food processor and pulse until the oats resemble fine oat bran. Set aside.

2. Preheat the oven to 375 degrees F.

3. In the bowl of a standing mixer fitted with the paddle attachment, combine the reserved oat flour, the remaining 3 cups oats, and the brown rice syrup, ¼ cup of the maple syrup, olive oil, salt, and vanilla until thoroughly combined, about 3 minutes.

4. Firmly press two-thirds of the dough onto a 9- by 12-inch baking sheet. Bake until light brown, about 15 minutes.

5. While the dough is baking, combine the berries, corn flour, and the remaining ¼ cup of the maple syrup in a medium-size bowl.

6. Evenly distribute the berry mixture over the baked oat crust. Crumble the remaining one-third of the dough over the berries, pressing it down firmly. Bake until a golden crust forms, about 40 minutes.

Pumpkin Glory Loaf

This loaf is rich in molasses and quite dark. The earthiness of the molasses and the autumn spices are warming and satisfying without being too sweet.

TWO 8½- BY 4½-INCH LOAVES, OR ONE 10-INCH SQUARE CAKE

    1 cup buckwheat flour

    2 cups brown rice flour

    1¾ teaspoons baking soda

    ¼ teaspoon salt

    1 teaspoon ground cinnamon

    1 teaspoon ground cloves

    1 cup safflower oil

    1 cup **molasses**

    1 cup **maple syrup**

    One 15-ounce can pumpkin puree, or approximately 1¾ cups cooked squash, sweet potato, or pumpkin

    1 teaspoon vanilla extract

    ½ cup chopped toasted walnuts

    ½ cup raisins

1. Preheat the oven to 375 degrees F.

2. Combine the buckwheat flour, brown rice flour, baking soda, salt, cinnamon, and cloves in a large bowl. In the bowl of a standing mixer fitted with the paddle attachment, combine the safflower oil, molasses, maple syrup, pumpkin, and vanilla until well mixed. With the mixer on low speed, add the flour mixture until well mixed, about 3 minutes. Fold in the walnuts and raisins.

3. Line the bottom of two 8½- by 4½-inch loaf pans or one 10-inch square cake pan with parchment paper, or grease and dust with brown rice flour. Pour in the batter.

4. Bake until the cake springs back when you press the center with your finger, about 50 minutes. Cool for about an hour before slicing.

Almond Cake

This cake works well as a sophisticated brunch or dessert offering. Though unfrosted, it is striking in appearance and delectable in taste.

ONE 10-INCH CAKE

    ¾ cup almonds

    2 cups brown rice flour

    ½ cup fava bean flour or chestnut flour

    2 teaspoons baking soda

    1 teaspoon sea salt

    ⅔ cup extra-virgin olive oil

    1½ cups water

    2 teaspoons vanilla extract

    1 teaspoon almond extract or amaretto

    1½ cups **maple syrup**

    1 cup sliced almonds

    1 cup sliced berries or cherries (optional)

    Powdered organic whole cane sugar (optional), for dusting the finished cake

1. Grind the almonds in a food processor until very fine. Set aside ½ cup, reserving any additional ground almonds for another use (store in an airtight container in the refrigerator or freezer).

2. Preheat the oven to 375 degrees F.

3. Combine the brown rice flour, fava bean flour, baking soda, and salt in a large bowl. In a separate large bowl, combine the olive oil, water, vanilla, almond extract, and maple syrup. Slowly whisk the flour mixture into the olive oil mixture until thoroughly combined.

4. Line the bottom of a 10-inch round springform pan with parchment paper, or grease and dust with brown rice flour. Pour in the batter. Decorate with the almonds and berries. Bake until the cake springs back when you press the center with your finger, or until a knife inserted in the center comes out clean, about 1 hour. Before serving, dust with powdered organic whole cane sugar.

Chapter 3

COOKIES

There is something so cheerful about making cookies at home. Here you will find takes on such comforting classics as Chocolate Chip Cookies (page 42) and Ginger Wheels (page 39), as well as fancier cookies such as Macaroons (page 53) and Russian Tea Cookies (page 41). I've also included some of my more revolutionary cookies, like the Stevia Wonders (page 51), Sweet Tahinis (page 46), and Honey Saffron Shortbread (page 45).

Cookies

Ginger Wheels (with Gingerbread People variation)

Russian Tea Cookies

Chocolate Chip Cookies (with Nut Butter Chocolate
Chip Cookies variation)

Honey Saffron Shortbread

Sweet Tahinis

Apricot Thumbprints

Maple "Butter" Bars

Stevia Wonders

Pumpkin Cookies

Macaroons

Chocolate Walnut Triangles

Hazelnut Honey Cookies

Ginger Wheels

This cookie is like a chewy molasses cookie but with the kick of ginger. Feel free to intensify the ginger flavor by adding more freshly grated gingerroot or to downplay it by adding less.

20 COOKIES

    4¼ cups brown rice flour

    1⅔ cups garbanzo bean flour or fava bean flour

    1 tablespoon baking powder

    ¾ teaspoon sea salt

    1 tablespoon ground ginger

    ¾ teaspoon ground cinnamon

    ½ teaspoon ground cloves

    1 tablespoon cocoa powder

    1½ cups canola oil

    1¼ cups **organic whole cane sugar**, plus more for sprinkling the cookies

    1 cup **molasses**

    1 tablespoon grated fresh gingerroot

    1 cup rice milk

    1 cup finely chopped candied ginger

1. Preheat the oven to 360 degrees F.

2. Combine the brown rice flour, garbanzo bean flour, baking powder, salt, ground ginger, cinnamon, cloves, and cocoa powder in a large bowl. In the bowl of a standing mixer fitted with the paddle attachment, combine the canola oil, organic whole cane sugar, molasses, gingerroot, and rice milk. With the mixer on low speed, add the flour mixture to the canola oil mixture until smooth.

3. Scoop the dough onto greased or parchment-lined baking sheets with an ice cream scoop. Gently press the dough balls down and score the tops with a fork to resemble spokes of a wheel. Sprinkle generously with organic whole cane sugar and bake until the edges are firm with a soft (but not sticky) center, about 15 minutes.

Gingerbread People

Have some fun with your gingerbread dough and create little people instead of the wheels.

1. For Gingerbread People, dust your counter liberally with brown rice flour. Roll out the dough to ½ inch thick and cut the dough with gingerbread people cookie cutters. Place the cutouts on the prepared baking sheets and decorate with whole cloves, raisins, or dairy-free chocolate chips for eyes and buttons. Bake until firm, about 17 minutes. After they have cooled, dress them up with Vanilla Frosting (page 94).

Russian Tea Cookies

Though I've altered it slightly, credit for this recipe belongs to Meghan, a wonderful baker who worked at Flying Apron years ago. These cookies are tender and melt in your mouth. They also look pretty on a platter.

18 COOKIES

> 2¼ cups brown rice flour
>
> 1 cup garbanzo bean flour or fava bean flour
>
> 1 cup finely ground pecans
>
> 2 cups palm oil or coconut oil
>
> 1⅓ cups **powdered organic whole cane sugar**, plus more for sprinkling cookies
>
> 2½ tablespoons **organic whole cane sugar**
>
> ¼ teaspoon sea salt
>
> ¾ teaspoon vanilla extract

1. Combine the brown rice flour, garbanzo bean flour, and pecans in a large bowl. In the bowl of a standing mixer fitted with the paddle attachment, combine the palm oil, powdered organic whole cane sugar, organic whole cane sugar, salt, and vanilla until well mixed. With the mixer on low speed, add the flour mixture a little at a time, until well mixed, about 3 minutes.

2. Scoop the dough onto prepared greased or parchment-lined baking sheets with an ice cream scoop. Freeze the cookies for at least 30 minutes or up to 1 week before baking.

3. Preheat the oven to 375 degrees F.

4. Bake the cookies until light brown, about 15 minutes.

5. Sift the powdered organic whole cane sugar and sprinkle over the top of the baked cookies while they are still hot. Wait until the cookies cool completely before transferring them from the baking sheets to a serving platter or cookie tin.

Chocolate Chip Cookies

Almost everyone delights in homemade chocolate chip cookies. I think the secret to truly great cookies is to use high-quality chocolate chips—in the bakery we use Dagoba dark chocolate. Chocolate chip cookies are really all about the chocolate!

25 COOKIES

    2¾ cups brown rice flour

    1½ cups plus 1 tablespoon garbanzo bean flour

    1 teaspoon baking powder

    ½ teaspoon baking soda

    ¾ teaspoon sea salt

    1 cup canola oil

    1 cup **organic whole cane sugar**

    1 teaspoon vanilla extract

    1 cup rice milk

    1 cup (8 ounces) dairy-free dark chocolate chips

    ¾ cup chopped nuts (optional)

    Cocoa powder, for dusting the cookies (optional)

1. Preheat the oven to 350 degrees F.

2. Combine the brown rice flour, garbanzo bean flour, baking powder, baking soda, and salt in a large bowl. In the bowl of a standing mixer fitted with the paddle attachment, combine the canola oil, organic whole cane sugar, and vanilla until well mixed. With the mixer on low speed, add the flour mixture and rice milk alternately, a little at a time, until smooth, about 3 minutes. Stir in the chocolate chips and nuts.

3. Scoop the dough onto greased or parchment-lined baking sheets with an ice cream scoop. Bake until golden and slightly firm to the touch, about 17 minutes. For a fancy look, dust the cookies with cocoa powder while they are still hot.

Nut Butter Chocolate Chip Cookies

For a twist on the standard chocolate chip cookies, try this nuttier variation. I love these because they satisfy my sweet tooth but aren't over-the-top sweet. I like to use peanut butter or almond butter, but pecan butter is terrific if you're in the mood for a splurge.

1. For Nut Butter Chocolate Chip Cookies, add ¾ cup nut butter into the mixer bowl along with the vanilla. Reduce the amount of chopped nuts to ½ cup.

Honey Saffron Shortbread

This recipe was created with the winter holidays in mind; however, this shortbread is great any time of year. The brightness of the honey and saffron adds warmth to a cool season.

12 COOKIES

> 1 cup coconut oil or palm oil
>
> ½ cup **honey**
>
> ⅛ teaspoon saffron
>
> ⅛ teaspoon salt
>
> 2 teaspoons vanilla extract
>
> 2 cups brown rice flour
>
> ½ cup ground toasted walnuts

1. Preheat the oven to 375 degrees F.

2. In the bowl of a standing mixer fitted with the paddle attachment, combine the coconut oil, honey, saffron, salt, and vanilla until well mixed. With the mixer on low speed, add the brown rice flour and mix until a smooth dough forms. Stir in the ground walnuts. *Note:* This is a very sticky dough.

3. Press the dough into a 10-inch tart pan or 9-inch square cake pan. Prick in several places with a fork. Bake until golden and firm to the touch, about 20 minutes.

4. While the shortbread is still hot, score it into 12 pieces with a knife. After the short-bread has cooled, slice it the rest of the way through.

To make shaped cookies: Chill the dough for 4 hours or overnight. Dust your counter liberally with brown rice flour. Roll out the dough to ⅝ inch thick and cut the dough with a floured cookie cutter. Transfer the cutouts to a greased baking sheet and bake until golden brown, approximately 20 minutes. Cool before transferring to a cookie tin or serving platter.

Sweet Tahinis

Here is a cookie that is reminiscent of halvah (a sweet sesame confection originating in the Middle East) but has the texture of a soft chewy cookie. Sesame butter, otherwise known as tahini, has a unique taste that most people love.

12 COOKIES

    2 cups brown rice flour

    1 teaspoon baking powder

    ½ teaspoon salt

    ½ cup tahini

    ½ cup palm oil or coconut oil

    1 cup **organic whole cane sugar**, plus more for sprinkling cookies

    1 teaspoon vanilla extract

    1 cup **agave syrup**

1. Preheat the oven to 375 degrees F.

2. Combine the brown rice flour, baking powder, and salt in a medium-size bowl. In the bowl of a standing mixer fitted with the paddle attachment, combine the tahini, palm oil, organic whole cane sugar, and vanilla until well mixed. With the mixer on low speed, add the flour mixture a little at a time until well mixed, about 3 minutes. Add the agave syrup and mix until combined.

3. Scoop the dough onto parchment-lined baking sheets with an ice cream scoop, dipping the scoop into water to avoid sticking. Indent each cookie with a fork mark and sprinkle with organic whole cane sugar. Bake until firm to the touch, about 17 minutes.

Apricot Thumbprints

This vanilla dough works well with many different thumbprint fillings, especially thick fruit jams. Your favorite store-bought jam will do, but if you prefer to make your own, The Joy of Cooking by Irma Rombauer has some wonderful recipes. Once you try the apricot filling that follows, though, you may find it hard to make these cookies any other way!

30 COOKIES

> 2¾ cups brown rice flour
>
> 1½ cups plus 1 tablespoon garbanzo bean flour
>
> 1 teaspoon baking powder
>
> ½ teaspoon baking soda
>
> ¾ teaspoon sea salt
>
> ½ teaspoon orange zest
>
> 1 cup canola oil
>
> 1 cup **organic whole cane sugar**, plus more for sprinkling the cookies
>
> 1 cup rice milk
>
> Apricot Puree (recipe follows)

1. Preheat the oven to 375 degrees F.

2. Combine the brown rice flour, garbanzo bean flour, baking powder, baking soda, salt, and orange zest in a large bowl. In the bowl of a standing mixer fitted with the paddle attachment, combine the canola oil and organic whole cane sugar until well mixed. With the mixer on low speed, add the flour mixture and rice milk alternately, a little at a time, until well mixed, about 3 minutes.

3. Scoop the cookie dough into Ping-Pong ball–sized mounds and place on greased or parchment-lined baking sheets, leaving 3 inches between the cookies. Make an indentation in the center of each cookie with the back of a wet spoon or with your thumb. Fill each indentation with a teaspoon of Apricot Puree or your favorite jam.

4. Sprinkle the edges of the cookies with organic whole cane sugar and bake until slightly firm to the touch, about 14 minutes.

Apricot Puree

     1½ cups dried apricots

     2 cups boiling water

     1 tablespoon freshly squeezed lemon juice

     2 teaspoons vanilla extract

     1½ tablespoons **organic whole cane sugar** (optional)

1. Place dried apricots in a large bowl and pour boiling water over them. Soak the apricots, covered, for 2 hours. Drain the apricots, reserving ¼ cup of the soaking liquid. Transfer the apricots and reserved soaking liquid to a food processor or blender. Puree until smooth. Blend in lemon juice, vanilla, and organic whole cane sugar.

Maple "Butter" Bars

These bars are very much like a rich shortbread. They've been a hit since we opened our doors.

12 COOKIES

2¾ cups brown rice flour

¼ teaspoon salt

1 cup coconut oil or palm oil

1 cup **maple syrup**

1 teaspoon vanilla extract

1. Preheat the oven to 375 degrees F.

2. Combine the brown rice flour and salt in a medium-size bowl. In the bowl of a standing mixer fitted with the paddle attachment, combine the coconut oil, maple syrup, and vanilla until well mixed. With the mixer on low speed, add the flour mixture a little at a time until well mixed, about 3 minutes.

3. Spread the batter evenly into a parchment-lined 9- by 12-inch baking pan. Bake until edges harden slightly, about 15 minutes. While the dough is still hot, score it into 12 pieces with a knife. After it has cooled, slice it the rest of the way through and remove the bars from the pan.

Stevia Wonders

This rich chocolaty dome cookie is sweetened with the stevia herb and dried apricots, making it ideal for those avoiding traditional sweeteners. You can find stevia at most health food stores; the powdered form is best for baking. The sweetness of the cocoa, the crunch of the nuts, and the richness of the texture makes eating these Stevia Wonders really satisfying.

12 COOKIES

> 1½ cups garbanzo bean flour
>
> ¾ cup cocoa powder
>
> 2 teaspoons ground cinnamon
>
> ½ teaspoon salt
>
> ¾ cup canola oil
>
> ¾ cup water
>
> 1 teaspoon vanilla extract
>
> ¾ teaspoon **powdered stevia**
>
> 1½ cups almonds, coarsely chopped, plus 12 whole almonds
>
> 1¾ cups dried apricots, coarsely chopped

1. Preheat the oven to 350 degrees F.

2. Combine the garbanzo bean flour, cocoa powder, cinnamon, and salt in a large bowl. In the bowl of a standing mixer fitted with the paddle attachment, combine the canola oil, water, vanilla, and powdered stevia until well mixed. With the mixer on low speed, add the flour mixture a little at a time until well mixed, about 3 minutes. Mix in the almonds and apricots.

3. Scoop the cookie dough into golf ball–sized domes and place on a greased or parchment-lined baking sheet. Lightly press a whole almond on top of each cookie and bake until slightly brown, about 12 minutes.

Pumpkin Cookies

This is a hearty snack for the health-conscious. Dried apricots and plump juicy raisins make this a very satisfying and sugar-free delight that goes great with a cup of tea.

15 COOKIES

>   1 cup buckwheat flour
>   ½ teaspoon ground cinnamon
>   ½ teaspoon ground cloves
>   ½ teaspoon nutmeg
>   ½ teaspoon ground ginger
>   6 tablespoons extra-virgin olive oil
>   ½ cup water
>   ½ teaspoon vanilla extract
>   ½ teaspoon **powdered stevia**
>   ½ cup pumpkin puree, canned or fresh
>   ¾ cup dried apricots, coarsely chopped
>   2 cups pecans, coarsely chopped, plus 12 whole pecans
>   ½ cup golden raisins (optional)

1. Preheat the oven to 350 degrees F.

2. Combine the buckwheat flour, cinnamon, cloves, nutmeg, and ginger in a medium-size bowl. In the bowl of a standing mixer fitted with the paddle attachment, combine the olive oil, water, vanilla, and powdered stevia until well mixed. With the mixer on low speed, add the flour mixture and pumpkin alternately, a little at a time, until well mixed, about 3 minutes. Add the apricots, pecans, and raisins, and mix until combined.

3. Scoop the cookie dough into golf ball–sized domes and place on a greased or parchment-lined baking sheet. Lightly press a whole pecan on top of each cookie and bake until slightly brown, 15 to 20 minutes.

Macaroons

Anyone who likes coconut will love this sweet treat. At the bakery we sometimes use the leftover chocolate sauce from this recipe to half-dip our chocolate chip cookies, or to drizzle atop a cake.

14 COOKIES

⅔ cup brown rice flour

5 cups shredded unsweetened coconut

½ teaspoon sea salt

⅔ cup **agave syrup**

1 cup coconut milk

2 teaspoons vanilla extract

Chocolate Sauce

1 cup (8 ounces) dairy-free dark chocolate chips or chopped dark chocolate

3 tablespoons water

2 tablespoons canola oil

1 teaspoon vanilla extract

Pinch sea salt

1. Preheat the oven to 350 degrees F.

2. Combine the rice flour, coconut, salt, agave syrup, coconut milk, and vanilla in a large bowl and mix thoroughly. The dough will be moist and slightly sticky.

3. Use an ice cream scoop to form the macaroons. Dip the scoop in a pitcher of water, then firmly pack the dough into the scoop just to the rim. (Packing the dough is critical so that the macaroons stay together when baked.) Ease the dough out of the scoop and onto a prepared greased or parchment-lined baking sheet. Repeat with the remaining dough. Bake until just barely brown, about 12 minutes.

4. While the cookies are baking, make the chocolate sauce. In a double boiler, or with a metal mixing bowl placed over a pot of simmering water, melt the chocolate chips, stirring frequently, 10 to 15 minutes. When chocolate has melted, whisk in the water, canola oil, vanilla, and salt until well combined. Remove from the heat.

5. Let the macaroons cool for 30 minutes on the baking sheets. Before serving, drizzle with the chocolate sauce. Leftover chocolate sauce can be stored in an airtight container in the fridge for up to 10 days. To use again, simply reheat in a double boiler.

Chocolate Walnut Triangles

This is one of the most indulgent goodies we make at Flying Apron; the rich, smooth choco-late wrapped around crunchy organic walnuts is an unforgettable combination. If you don't have walnuts on hand, pecans and almonds work equally well in these cookies.

12 COOKIES

> ¼ cup palm oil or coconut oil
>
> 1 cup (8 ounces) dairy-free dark chocolate chips
>
> 1 teaspoon vanilla extract
>
> ⅛ teaspoon sea salt
>
> 1 cup chopped toasted walnuts

1. In a double boiler, or with a metal mixing bowl placed over a pot of simmering water, melt the palm oil and chocolate, stirring frequently. Remove from the heat and stir in the vanilla, salt, and walnuts.

2. Pour the mixture into a parchment-lined 9-inch round cake pan or fudge molds. Transfer to the refrigerator to set, 1 hour.

3. Once the chocolate is firm, remove from the pan and slice into wedges with a knife that has been dipped in hot water. If using fudge molds, simply remove the chocolate from the molds. Store any leftovers in an airtight container in the freezer for 14 days.

Hazelnut Honey Cookies

We love this cookie at Flying Apron because we make it with all regional (Pacific Northwest), organic ingredients. Rich, toasty hazelnut flour and flavorful Northwest honey—can you think of a better combination?

15 COOKIES

>2 cups hazelnut flour
>
>1 cup **honey**
>
>¼ teaspoon sea salt
>
>1 teaspoon vanilla extract
>
>1 teaspoon dried lavender or dried rosemary
>
>15 Rainier or Bing cherries (fresh or frozen), pitted

1. Preheat the oven to 350 degrees F.

2. Combine the hazelnut flour, honey, salt, vanilla, and lavender in a large bowl. Mix until smooth.

3. Scoop the cookie dough into Ping-Pong ball–sized mounds and place on a greased or parchment-lined baking sheet. Lightly press a cherry on top of each cookie and bake until firm to the touch, about 20 minutes.

Chapter 4

PIES AND TARTS

I would like to thank our ancestors who were responsible for bringing to life the beautiful combination of soft, sweet fruits and tender crust. For centuries, cultures around the globe have been engaging in the art of pie- and tart-making. In this chapter, you will learn how to join in the tradition—although many of the ingredients called for are far from traditional.

Pie Crusts

Standard Pie Crust

Cornmeal Pine Nut Pie Crust

Almond Pie Crust

Pie Fillings

Mixed Berry Pie

Pumpkin Pie

Old-Fashioned Apple Pie

Pecan Pie

Cherry Pie with Almond Crust

Peach Walnut Tart

Cranberry Tart with Orange Zest

Pie Crusts

Because there is no gluten in these pie crusts, you don't have to worry about overmixing. In fact, you may find them much easier to work with than traditional pie crusts. Do note that while these pie crusts are deliciously tender and beautiful, you may find top crusts to be somewhat less sturdy than a traditional crust when serving.

These recipes provide a generous amount of dough, so after you have formed your crust, you may find that you have some left over. I like to use any leftover dough to make cutouts to decorate the top of the unbaked pie crust. Another option is to roll extra dough out, cut it into cookie shapes, sprinkle with cinnamon and sugar, and bake alongside the pie until the cookies are slightly browned, about 12 minutes.

Standard Pie Crust

This pie dough is a pleasure to work with and will be like no crust you've ever tasted. It has just the right balance of flakiness and richness.

Single Crust

> 1½ cups brown rice flour
>
> ¼ teaspoon sea salt
>
> ½ cup plus 3 tablespoons palm oil or coconut oil
>
> 3 tablespoons **agave syrup**, **maple syrup**, or **concentrated fruit juice** (I recommend Mystic Lake Dairy's pineapple-peach-pear juice concentrate)
>
> 1 to 2 tablespoons cold water

Double Crust

> 3 cups brown rice flour
>
> ½ teaspoon sea salt
>
> 1½ cups palm oil or coconut oil
>
> ¼ cup plus 2 tablespoons **agave syrup**, **maple syrup**, or **concentrated fruit juice**
>
> 2 to 3 tablespoons cold water

1. Combine the brown rice flour and salt in a large bowl. In the bowl of a standing mixer fitted with the paddle attachment, mix the palm oil until softened, about 1 minute. With the mixer on low speed, add the flour mixture slowly until incorporated. Add the agave syrup and water and mix until a soft dough has formed, about 5 minutes. If the dough is dry, add additional water 1 tablespoon at a time until the dough is smooth.

2. For a double-crust pie, set aside and cover half of the dough. There is no need to refrigerate it.

3. Dust your work surface (a 12- by 18-inch cutting board or piece of cardboard covered in parchment paper works well) and your hands liberally with brown rice flour. Place the dough on your work surface and sprinkle the top with more brown rice flour. Roll the dough into an 11-inch disc.

4. Place your pie plate on top of the rolled-out dough. With one hand under the work surface and the other on the pie plate, flip them so that the cutting board is on top. Set the pie plate on the counter, remove the cutting board, and gently press the pie dough into the pie plate. Any tears that occur can be fixed by gently pressing and pinching the dough back together.

5. For a single-crust pie, decoratively flute the perimeter of the pie crust by pressing a fork along the edge or using your thumb and forefinger to pinch the edge.

6. For a double-crust pie, roll out the second half of the crust in the same manner. After adding filling to the bottom crust, slide the top crust onto the pie. Seal the perimeter by pressing a fork along the edge or using your thumb and forefinger to pinch the edge over the par-baked bottom crust.

Cornmeal Pine Nut Pie Crust

This Italian-inspired pie dough is rich in flavor with the addition of ground pine nuts.

Single Crust

¾ cup brown rice flour

½ cup cornmeal

¼ cup ground pine nuts

¼ teaspoon sea salt

½ cup plus 2 tablespoons palm oil

2 tablespoons **agave syrup**, **maple syrup**, or **concentrated fruit juice** (I recommend Mystic Lake Dairy's pineapple-peach-pear juice concentrate)

1 to 2 tablespoons cold water

Double Crust

1½ cups brown rice flour

1 cup cornmeal

½ cup ground pine nuts

½ teaspoon sea salt

1¼ cup palm oil

¼ cup **agave syrup**, **maple syrup**, or **concentrated fruit juice**

2 to 3 tablespoons cold water

1. Combine the brown rice flour, cornmeal, pine nuts, and salt in a large bowl. In the bowl of a standing mixer fitted with the paddle attachment, mix the palm oil until softened, about 1 minute. With the mixer on low speed, add the flour mixture slowly until just incorporated. Add the agave syrup and water and mix until a soft dough has formed, about 5 minutes. If the dough is dry, add additional water 1 tablespoon at a time until the dough is smooth.

2. For a double-crust pie, set aside and cover half of the dough. There is no need to refrigerate it.

3. Dust your work surface (a 12- by 18-inch cutting board or piece of cardboard covered in parchment paper works well) and your hands liberally with brown rice flour. Place the dough on your work surface and sprinkle the top with more brown rice flour. Roll the dough into an 11-inch disc.

4. Place your pie plate on top of the rolled-out dough. With one hand under the work surface and the other on the pie plate, flip them so that the cutting board is on top. Set the pie plate on the counter, remove the cutting board, and gently press the pie dough into the pie plate. Any tears that occur can be fixed by gently pressing and pinching the dough back together.

5. For a single-crust pie, decoratively flute the perimeter of the pie crust by pressing a fork along the edge or using your thumb and forefinger to pinch the edge.

6. For a double-crust pie, roll out the second half of the crust in the same manner. After adding filling to the bottom crust, slide the top crust onto the pie. Seal the perimeter by pressing a fork along the edge or using your thumb and forefinger to pinch the edge over the par-baked bottom crust.

Almond Pie Crust

This sweet and nutty dough is a perfect foundation for any pie you want to fancy-up a bit. And the honey helps give this dough a wonderful consistency that's easy to work with.

Single Crust

> 1¼ cups brown rice flour
>
> ¼ cup almond meal
>
> ⅛ teaspoon sea salt
>
> ½ cup plus 3 tablespoons palm oil
>
> 3 tablespoons **honey**
>
> ¼ teaspoon almond extract
>
> 1 tablespoon cold water

Double Crust

> 2½ cups brown rice flour
>
> ½ cup almond meal
>
> ¼ teaspoon sea salt
>
> 1¼ cups plus 2 tablespoons palm oil
>
> ¼ cup plus 2 tablespoons **honey**
>
> ½ teaspoon almond extract
>
> 2 to 3 tablespoons cold water

1. Combine the brown rice flour, almond meal, and salt in a large bowl. In the bowl of a standing mixer fitted with the paddle attachment, mix the palm oil until softened, about 1 minute. With the mixer on low speed, add the flour mixture slowly until just incorporated. Add the honey, almond extract, and water and mix until a soft dough has formed, about 5 minutes. If the dough is dry, add additional water 1 tablespoon at a time until the dough is smooth.

2. For a double-crust pie, set aside and cover half of the dough. There is no need to refrigerate it.

3. Dust your work surface (a 12- by 18-inch cutting board or piece of cardboard covered in parchment paper works well) and your hands liberally with brown rice flour. Place the dough on your work surface and sprinkle the top with more brown rice flour. Roll the dough into an 11-inch disc.

4. Place your pie plate on top of the rolled-out dough. With one hand under the work surface and the other on the pie plate, flip them so that the cutting board is on top. Set the pie plate on the counter, remove the cutting board, and gently press the pie dough into the pie plate. Any tears that occur can be fixed by gently pressing and pinching the dough back together.

5. For a single-crust pie, decoratively flute the perimeter of the pie crust by pressing a fork along the edge or using your thumb and forefinger to pinch the edge.

6. For a double-crust pie, roll out the second half of the crust in the same manner. After adding filling to the bottom crust, slide the top crust onto the pie. Seal the perimeter by pressing a fork along the edge or using your thumb and forefinger to pinch the edge over the par-baked bottom crust.

Pie Fillings

Pies fillings are fun to experiment with and can be quite unique, not to mention colorful and textured. Try pairing the different fillings here with the various pie crusts—you may discover a favorite combination that will have people clamoring for your one-of-a-kind pie!

Mixed Berry Pie

A little bit of sweetness mixed with the natural tartness of berries makes this a refreshingly zesty treat. Because the berries are the highlight of this pie, I prefer to use Standard Pie Crust (page 62) for this recipe.

ONE 9-INCH PIE

> 3 cups fresh blueberries
>
> 3 cups fresh raspberries or blackberries
>
> 1 teaspoon ground cinnamon
>
> 3 tablespoons arrowroot powder
>
> ⅓ cup **maple syrup** or **concentrated fruit juice** (I recommend Mystic Lake Dairy's pineapple-peach-pear juice concentrate)
>
> 1 tablespoon freshly squeezed lemon juice
>
> 1 double *unbaked* pie crust

1. Preheat the oven to 375 degrees F.

2. In a large mixing bowl, combine the berries, cinnamon, and arrowroot powder. Mix gently until the berries are well coated. Add the maple syrup and lemon juice and toss gently, being careful not to overmix.

3. Prepare a 9-inch pie plate with the bottom crust (see instructions on page 63). Par-bake the bottom pie crust for 15 minutes, ideally on a preheated pizza stone.

4. Decrease the oven temperature to 350 degrees F.

5. Spoon the berry filling into the par-baked bottom crust. Roll out the remaining pie dough, place it on top of the filling, and crimp the edge over the bottom crust (see instructions on page 63). Cut four small slits in the center of the top of the pie to provide space for steam to escape.

6. Bake on the bottom rack of the oven until the berries begin to bubble and solidify and the crust is light brown, about 50 minutes. Check the pie halfway through; if it is browning too quickly, cover it with foil. Cool slightly before serving.

Pumpkin Pie

This rich and flavorful pie will warm your heart on those chilly fall days. Around the holidays, we make hundreds of these pies for our customers.

ONE 9-INCH PIE

One 15-ounce can pumpkin puree, or approximately 1¾ cups cooked pumpkin

½ cup Apricot Puree (see page 49)

½ teaspoon sea salt

¾ tablespoon arrowroot powder

1¼ teaspoons ground cinnamon

¼ teaspoon ground ginger

¼ teaspoon ground nutmeg

½ teaspoon vanilla extract

4 tablespoons **brown rice syrup**

6 tablespoons **maple syrup**

¾ cup rice milk or almond milk

1 single *unbaked* pie crust

1. Preheat the oven to 350 degrees F.

2. Combine the pumpkin puree, apricot puree, salt, arrowroot powder, cinnamon, ginger, nutmeg, vanilla, brown rice syrup, maple syrup, and rice milk in a large bowl until smooth.

3. Prepare a 9-inch pie plate with the crust (see instructions on page 63). Par-bake the pie crust for 15 minutes, ideally on a preheated pizza stone.

4. Pour the pumpkin filling into the par-baked crust. Bake on the bottom rack of the oven until the filling is puffed around the edges and the center has set, about 50 minutes. Check the pie halfway through; if the crust is browning too quickly, cover it with foil. Cool before serving.

Old-Fashioned Apple Pie

Everyone loves a good homemade apple pie, and this is a recipe you can depend on. Not overly sweetened, this recipe highlights the natural sweetness of the apples. Golden Delicious, Granny Smith, and Honeycrisp apples are wonderful in pies, and it is fun to combine varieties in one pie for a more complex, interesting flavor. Be sure to pile those apples high; they will bake down considerably in the oven.

ONE 9-INCH PIE

> 5 medium apples, peeled, cored, and sliced
>
> ½ cup golden raisins (optional)
>
> 1 teaspoon ground cinnamon
>
> 1 tablespoon arrowroot powder
>
> ⅓ cup **maple syrup**
>
> 1 tablespoon freshly squeezed lemon juice
>
> 1 tablespoon vanilla extract
>
> 1 double *unbaked* pie crust

1. Preheat the oven to 375 degrees F.

2. In a large mixing bowl, combine the apples, raisins, cinnamon, and arrowroot powder until the apples are well coated. Add the maple syrup, lemon juice, and vanilla and toss well.

3. Prepare a 9-inch pie plate with the bottom crust (see instructions on page 63). Par-bake the bottom pie crust for 15 minutes, ideally on a preheated pizza stone.

4. Decrease the oven temperature to 350 degrees F.

5. Spoon the apple filling into the par-baked bottom crust. Roll out the remaining pie dough, place it on top of the filling, and crimp the edge over the bottom crust (see instructions on page 63). Cut four small slits in the center of the top of the pie to provide space for steam to escape.

6. Bake on the bottom rack of the oven until the apples and juices are bubbling and beginning to solidify, about 50 minutes. The crust should be a nice golden brown. Check the pie halfway through; if it is browning too quickly, cover it with foil. Cool slightly before serving.

Pecan Pie

The beautiful pecans and deep flavors of maple syrup make this one of our most tempting pies. Make sure you have friends around to share it with; this rich and decadent pie really goes a long way.

ONE 9-INCH PIE

> ¼ cup plus 2 tablespoons **brown rice syrup**
>
> ¾ cup **maple syrup**
>
> 1½ tablespoons arrowroot powder
>
> ¾ teaspoon ground cinnamon
>
> 3 tablespoons almond butter
>
> 3¾ cups coarsely chopped pecans, plus 3 whole pecans for decorating the top of the pie
>
> 1 single *unbaked* pie crust

1. Preheat the oven to 375 degrees F.

2. In the bowl of a standing mixer fitted with the paddle attachment, combine the brown rice syrup, maple syrup, arrowroot powder, cinnamon, and almond butter until very well mixed, about 3 minutes. Mix in the pecans.

3. Prepare a 9-inch pie plate with the crust (see instructions on page 63). Par-bake the pie crust for 15 minutes, ideally on a preheated pizza stone.

4. Pour the pecan filling into the par-baked crust. Place the whole pecans decoratively in the center of the top of the pie. Bake on the bottom rack of the oven until the filling is almost set, about 40 minutes. Check the pie halfway through; if the crust is browning too quickly, cover it with foil. Cool before serving.

Cherry Pie with Almond Crust

Sweet cherries and almonds are a classic combination; the two come together in this pie to form a match made in heaven.

ONE 9-INCH PIE

> 6 cups fresh or frozen cherries, pitted
>
> 1 teaspoon ground cinnamon
>
> 3 tablespoons arrowroot powder
>
> ⅓ cup **maple syrup**
>
> 1 tablespoon freshly squeezed lemon juice
>
> 1 double *unbaked* Almond Pie Crust (page 66)

1. Preheat the oven to 375 degrees F.

2. In a large mixing bowl, combine the cherries, cinnamon, and arrowroot powder until the cherries are well coated. Add the maple syrup and lemon juice and toss well.

3. Prepare a 9-inch pie plate with the bottom crust (see instructions on page 67). Par-bake the bottom pie crust for 15 minutes, ideally on a preheated pizza stone.

4. Spoon the cherry filling into the par-baked bottom crust. Roll out the remaining pie dough, place it on top of the filling, and crimp the edge over the bottom crust (see instructions on page 67). Cut four small slits in the center of the top of the pie to provide space for steam to escape.

5. Bake on the bottom rack of the oven until the crust is golden brown, about 50 minutes. Cool slightly before serving.

Peach Walnut Tart

This tart is best in summer when peaches are at their peak. The concentric circles of peach slices are beautiful, and the flavor is magnificent.

ONE 10-INCH TART

4 peaches, peeled, pitted, and sliced into thin wedges

1 teaspoon ground cinnamon

3 tablespoons arrowroot powder

⅓ cup **maple syrup** or **concentrated fruit juice** (I recommend Mystic Lake Dairy's pineapple-peach-pear juice concentrate)

2 tablespoons brandy, or 1 tablespoon freshly squeezed lemon juice

½ cup ground walnuts (optional)

Powdered organic whole cane sugar (optional), for dusting

1 single *unbaked* pie crust

1. Preheat the oven to 375 degrees F.

2. In a large mixing bowl, combine the peaches, cinnamon, and arrowroot powder. Mix gently until the peaches are well coated. Add the maple syrup and brandy and toss gently, being careful not to overmix.

3. Prepare a 10-inch tart pan with the crust (see instructions on page 63). Par-bake the crust for 15 minutes, ideally on a preheated pizza stone.

4. Arrange the coated peaches in concentric circles on the par-baked crust, filling the tart pan snugly. Pour any remaining liquid over the top of the peaches. Sprinkle with the ground walnuts.

5. Bake on the bottom rack of the oven until filling is set and peaches cooked through, about 45 minutes. Check the tart halfway through; if it is browning too quickly, cover it with foil. Cool slightly before serving.

6. Dust the edges of the tart with powdered organic whole cane sugar.

Cranberry Tart with Orange Zest

A beautiful fall treat, this tart combines the pleasant tartness of cranberry with the sweetness of apple and maple syrup. It makes a memorable end to a fancy meal.

ONE 10-INCH TART

> 3 cups diced, peeled apples
>
> 2 cups fresh or frozen cranberries
>
> 1 teaspoon orange zest
>
> 1 teaspoon ground cinnamon
>
> 3 tablespoons arrowroot powder
>
> ½ cup **maple syrup**
>
> ½ tablespoon freshly squeezed lemon juice
>
> 1 single *unbaked* Cornmeal Pine Nut Pie Crust (page 64)
>
> ½ cup apricot jam

1. Preheat the oven to 375 degrees F.

2. In a large mixing bowl, combine the apples, cranberries, orange zest, cinnamon, and arrowroot powder. Mix until the apples and cranberries are well coated. Add the maple syrup and lemon juice, and toss well.

3. Prepare a 10-inch tart pan with the crust (see instructions on page 65). Par-bake the crust for 15 minutes, ideally on a preheated pizza stone.

4. Spoon the filling into the par-baked crust.

5. Bake on the bottom rack of the oven until the filling is set and the apples cooked through, about 50 minutes. Check the crust halfway through; if it is browning too quickly, cover it with foil.

6. While the tart is baking, warm the apricot jam in a double boiler, or with a metal mixing bowl placed over a pot of simmering water, until it becomes thin, about 10 minutes. Strain the heated jam into a small bowl. Let the tart cool slightly and gently drizzle or brush the glaze over the top.

Chapter 5

Cakes, Cupcakes, and Frostings

Cakes are a must at any special occasion, and even a regular day that includes cake suddenly becomes transformed. While baking and frosting a cake from scratch is a bit time-consuming, it's easier than you might think, and becomes even easier the more often you practice. In fact, as the French would say, "C'est du gâteau!" ("It's a piece of cake!")

Before making your cake, be sure to review the "Assembling Your Cake" section on page 84, as assembly instructions are not included in the individual recipes. Also, for each cake recipe I've suggested a type of frosting to go with the cake, but I encourage you to experiment with different combinations—maybe you'll even come up with a combination we've never thought of at Flying Apron!

Cakes and Cupcakes
Cardamom Spice Cake
Maple Cake
Coconut Heaven Cake
Dark Chocolate Cake
Mexican Chocolate Cake
Carrot Cake

Frostings
Vanilla Frosting (with Lemon Frosting, Amaretto Frosting,
and White Rum Frosting variations)
Dark Chocolate Ganache Frosting
German Maple Frosting
Chai "Buttercream" Frosting
Coconut Heaven Frosting
Agave-Sweetened Lemon Frosting
Nut Butter Frosting
Rose Tea–Infused Frosting

Cakes and Cupcakes

All of the following recipes can be enjoyed either as cakes or as cupcakes (use 3-inch tins for best results). When frosting cupcakes, experiment with different tips on a piping bag. Try starting on the perimeter of a cupcake and swirling toward the center, creating an effect like soft-serve ice cream. Or simply spread the frosting on each cupcake with a butter knife and top with an edible flower, chopped nuts, shaved chocolate, candied lemon zest, or fresh mint. Use your imagination and have fun!

Assembling Your Cake

All of the cake recipes in this chapter are for three-layer cakes. If you've never put together a layer cake before, or if you need a quick refresher, please read on.

Begin with completely cooled cakes. Novices might find it helpful to freeze the cake layers overnight. Make sure to wrap the cake layers very tightly with plastic wrap to prevent them from drying out.

Place the bottom cake layer on a serving platter, cardboard cake round, or decorating pedestal. Place enough frosting on the cake layer to evenly cover the surface, about ¾ cup. Spread the frosting with a frosting spatula or butter knife, making sure you frost the cake all the way to the edges. If the recipe calls for a layer of fruit or jam, add that next, leaving about an inch of the perimeter untouched by the fruit filling. Place the second cake layer on top of the first and repeat with the frosting (and fruit or jam, if using). Set the third cake layer on top.

Next, frost the exterior of the cake. Using your spatula or butter knife, cover the sides of the cake with a layer of frosting. Once the sides are covered, go back and smooth the frosting. Dip a firm metal spatula or frosting spreader in a container of boiling hot water every so often while smoothing the exterior surface. Follow the same process to frost the top of the cake.

Once your cake is frosted, you can further decorate it by using a piping bag to draw a simple border of frosting around the top and bottom perimeters of the cake. Even a sturdy plastic storage bag can work; simply scoop frosting into the bag, cut a small piece of one corner off, and use it to create pearls or polka dots of frosting. Dress your cake up further by drizzling melted chocolate or sprinkling toasted coconut on top. Even edible fresh organic flowers can be festive cake decorations.

Cardamom Spice Cake

This is the cake that made Flying Apron popular when we first opened. Reminiscent of an old-fashioned spice cake, it takes on extra pizzazz with Chai "Buttercream" Frosting (page 99).

ONE 9-INCH THREE-LAYER CAKE OR 33 CUPCAKES

>   4 cups brown rice flour
>
>   2 cups garbanzo bean flour, sifted
>
>   1 tablespoon plus 1 teaspoon baking soda
>
>   1 teaspoon sea salt
>
>   ½ teaspoon ground cinnamon
>
>   2 teaspoons ground cardamom
>
>   1⅓ cups extra-virgin olive oil or canola oil
>
>   3 cups water
>
>   1 teaspoon apple cider vinegar
>
>   1 tablespoon plus 1 teaspoon vanilla extract
>
>   3 cups **agave syrup**, **maple syrup**, or **concentrated pear juice**

1. Preheat the oven to 350 degrees F.

2. Line the bottoms of three 9-inch cake pans with parchment paper. Set aside.

3. Combine the brown rice flour, garbanzo bean flour, baking soda, salt, cinnamon, and cardamom in a large bowl. In a separate large bowl, combine the olive oil, water, apple cider vinegar, vanilla, and agave syrup. Slowly whisk the flour mixture into the olive oil mixture until thoroughly combined.

4. Pour the batter into the prepared pans and bake until the cake springs back when you press the center with your finger, about 30 minutes. Once the cake has cooled and you have prepared a frosting, assemble following the instructions on page 84.

    For cupcakes: Divide the batter evenly among 33 lined cupcake tin cups. Bake until a toothpick inserted in the center comes out clean, about 15 minutes.

Maple Cake

This cake is particularly good when used to make an Apricot Bliss Cake. To make an Apricot Bliss Cake, you will need a batch of Apricot Puree (page 49), as well as a batch of Vanilla Frosting (page 94). Follow the directions for jam-filled cakes (see instructions on page 84). For a rich pairing, this cake is also delicious with Dark Chocolate Ganache Frosting (page 96).

ONE 9-INCH THREE-LAYER CAKE OR 33 CUPCAKES

> 4 cups brown rice flour
>
> 2 cups garbanzo bean flour
>
> 1 tablespoon plus 1 teaspoon baking soda
>
> 1 teaspoon sea salt
>
> 1⅓ cups canola oil or extra-virgin olive oil
>
> 3 cups water
>
> 1 tablespoon plus 1 teaspoon vanilla extract
>
> 3 cups **maple syrup**

1. Preheat the oven to 350 degrees F.

2. Line the bottoms of three 9-inch cake pans with parchment paper. Set aside.

3. Combine the brown rice flour, garbanzo bean flour, baking soda, and salt in a large bowl. In a separate large bowl, combine the canola oil, water, vanilla, and maple syrup. Slowly whisk the flour mixture into the canola oil mixture until thoroughly combined.

4. Pour the batter into the prepared pans and bake until the cake springs back when you press the center with your finger, about 30 minutes. Once the cake has cooled and you have prepared a frosting, assemble following the instructions on page 84.

   For cupcakes: Divide the batter evenly among 33 lined cupcake tin cups. Bake until a toothpick inserted into the center comes out clean, about 15 minutes.

Coconut Heaven Cake

This cake is bursting with coconut and very satisfying. It should be frosted with our Coconut Heaven Frosting (page 100). You can also add finely chopped pineapple between the layers.

ONE 9-INCH THREE-LAYER CAKE OR 33 CUPCAKES

    4 cups brown rice flour

    2 cups garbanzo bean flour

    1 tablespoon plus 1 teaspoon baking soda

    1 teaspoon sea salt

    1⅓ cups canola oil

    3 cups water

    1 teaspoon apple cider vinegar

    1 tablespoon plus 1 teaspoon vanilla extract

    3 cups **agave syrup** or **concentrated fruit juice** (I recommend Mystic Lake Dairy's pineapple-peach-pear juice concentrate)

    3 cups shredded toasted coconut

1. Preheat the oven to 350 degrees F.

2. Line the bottoms of three 9-inch cake pans with parchment paper. Set aside.

3. Combine the brown rice flour, garbanzo bean flour, baking soda, and salt in a large bowl. In a separate large bowl, combine the canola oil, water, apple cider vinegar, vanilla, and agave syrup. Slowly whisk the flour mixture into the canola oil mixture until thoroughly combined.

4. Pour the batter into the prepared pans and bake until the cake springs back when you press the center with your finger, about 30 minutes. Once the cake has cooled and you have prepared a frosting, assemble following the instructions on page 84.

   For cupcakes: Divide the batter evenly among 33 lined cupcake tin cups. Bake until a toothpick inserted into the center comes out clean, about 15 minutes.

Dark Chocolate Cake

I love the really dark chocolate flavor and the moistness of this cake. Try pairing it with Vanilla Frosting (page 94) or Amaretto Frosting (page 95), or layering it with some fresh berries. The layers for this cake are made thinner than some of the others because this cake is so rich.

ONE 9-INCH THREE-LAYER CAKE OR 25 CUPCAKES

> 1¾ cups brown rice flour
>
> ¾ cup garbanzo bean or chestnut flour, sifted
>
> 1⅓ cups sifted cocoa powder
>
> 1 tablespoon baking soda
>
> 1½ teaspoons sea salt
>
> 1 cup extra-virgin olive oil or canola oil
>
> 2 cups water
>
> 2 cups **maple syrup**

1. Preheat the oven to 350 degrees F.

2. Line the bottoms of three 9-inch cake pans with parchment paper. Set aside.

3. Combine the brown rice flour, garbanzo bean flour, cocoa powder, baking soda, and salt in a large bowl. In a separate large bowl, combine the olive oil, water, and maple syrup. Slowly whisk the flour mixture into the olive oil mixture until thoroughly combined.

4. Pour the batter into the prepared pans and bake until the cake springs back when you press the center with your finger, about 25 minutes. Once the cake has cooled and you have prepared a frosting, assemble following the instructions on page 84.

   For cupcakes: Divide the batter evenly among 25 lined cupcake tin cups. Bake until a toothpick inserted into the center comes out clean, about 15 minutes.

Mexican Chocolate Cake

This spicy chocolate cake boasts hints of cinnamon and cayenne that will have you saying "Qué bueno!" in no time! Pair this with the Dark Chocolate Ganache Frosting (page 96).

ONE 9-INCH THREE-LAYER CAKE OR 25 CUPCAKES

  1¾ cups brown rice flour

  ¾ cup garbanzo bean flour or chestnut flour, sifted

  1⅓ cups cocoa powder, sifted

  1 tablespoon baking soda

  1½ teaspoons sea salt

  ¾ teaspoon ground cinnamon

  ⅛ teaspoon cayenne

  1 cup extra-virgin olive oil or canola oil

  1¾ cups water

  2 cups **maple syrup**

  1 banana, mashed

1. Preheat the oven to 350 degrees F.

2. Line the bottoms of three 9-inch cake pans with parchment paper. Set aside.

3. Combine the brown rice flour, garbanzo bean flour, cocoa powder, baking soda, salt, cinnamon, and cayenne in a large bowl. In a separate large bowl, combine the olive oil, water, maple syrup, and mashed banana. Slowly whisk the flour mixture into the olive oil mixture until thoroughly combined.

4. Pour the batter into the prepared pans and bake until the cake springs back when you press the center with your finger, about 25 minutes. Once the cake has cooled and you have prepared a frosting, assemble following the instructions on page 84.

   For cupcakes: Divide the batter evenly among 25 lined cupcake tin cups. Bake until a toothpick inserted into the center comes out clean, about 15 minutes.

Carrot Cake

This sweet, moist cake is full of tasty morsels—chewy pieces of coconut, sweet bursts of raisins, and crunchy walnut pieces create a tantalizing symphony in your mouth. This cake is delicious with our Vanilla Frosting (page 94), but for a completely alternatively sweetened cake, try Coconut Heaven Frosting (page 100), Agave-Sweetened Lemon Frosting (page 101), or German Maple Frosting (page 97). This cake is also delicious when layered with frosting and Apricot Puree (page 49).

ONE 9-INCH THREE-LAYER CAKE

> 2 cups brown rice flour
>
> 1¼ cups garbanzo bean flour or chestnut flour
>
> 1½ teaspoons baking soda
>
> ¾ teaspoon sea salt
>
> 1½ teaspoons ground cinnamon
>
> 1 cup canola oil
>
> 2 cups water
>
> 1 tablespoon vanilla extract
>
> 2 cups **agave syrup**, **maple syrup**, or **concentrated fruit juice** (I recommend Mystic Lake Dairy's pineapple-peach-pear juice concentrate)
>
> 5 medium carrots, grated (about 1¼ cups)
>
> 2½ cups shredded unsweetened coconut
>
> 2 cups chopped walnuts or pecans
>
> 1 cup golden raisins

1. Preheat the oven to 350 degrees F.

2. Line the bottoms of three 9-inch cake pans with parchment paper. Set aside.

3. Combine the brown rice flour, garbanzo bean flour, baking soda, salt, and cinnamon in a large bowl. In a second large bowl, combine the canola oil, water, vanilla, and agave syrup. In a third large bowl, combine the carrots, coconut, walnuts, and

raisins. Slowly whisk the flour mixture into the canola oil mixture until thoroughly combined. Fold in the carrot mixture until combined.

4. Pour the batter into the prepared pans and bake until a toothpick inserted into the center comes out clean, about 40 minutes. Once the cake has cooled and you have prepared a frosting, assemble following the instructions on page 84.

Frostings

Frosting cakes is a lot of fun. It's not necessary to have a lot of fancy tools, but a few can aid in the process. A spinning cake pedestal, frosting spatula (a thin, long spatula with a long handle), and piping bag are my favorite tools. However, if all you have is a plate, a butter knife, and a plastic storage bag, not to worry—your cake can still be delicious and beautiful.

Vanilla Frosting

This frosting is a classic. The rich and creamy vanilla flavor is a perfect complement to any cake. I particularly like it with Dark Chocolate Cake (page 88). It's a classic pairing loved by young and old alike.

ENOUGH FROSTING FOR ONE 9-INCH THREE-LAYER CAKE

 2 cups palm oil

 6⅔ cups **powdered organic whole cane sugar**, sifted

 ¼ teaspoon sea salt

 ½ cup boiling water

 ½ cup **agave syrup** or **concentrated fruit juice** (I recommend Mystic Lake Dairy's pineapple-peach-pear juice concentrate)

 2 tablespoons vanilla extract

1. In the bowl of a standing mixer fitted with the paddle attachment, beat the palm oil and powdered organic whole cane sugar until soft. With the mixer on low speed, add the salt, boiling water, agave syrup, and vanilla. Continue to beat, scraping the sides of the bowl occasionally, until smooth and fluffy. To achieve the desired consistency, turn the mixer to high speed for 2 to 3 minutes.

2. Use right away, or store in an airtight container in the refrigerator for up to 1 week. When you are ready to use the frosting, warm it slightly in a double boiler, or with a metal mixing bowl placed over a pot of simmering water, and whip it again until it is fluffy.

Lemon Frosting

A refreshing twist on our classic Vanilla Frosting, this lemony indulgence adds an extra burst of flavor to any cake you choose to pair it with.

1. For Lemon Frosting, add ¼ teaspoon lemon oil and the zest of 1 lemon.

Amaretto Frosting

The sophisticated flavor of almond liqueur in this frosting makes a wonderful accompaniment to a simple cake. This frosting will be the highlight of your dessert, and it goes great with a cup of coffee or espresso.

1. For Amaretto Frosting, simply add ½ teaspoon amaretto or almond extract.

White Rum Frosting

This frosting adds warmth and tingle to an already smooth white frosting.

1. For White Rum Frosting, simply replace ¼ cup of the agave syrup with ¼ cup of white rum.

Dark Chocolate Ganache Frosting

This is a great recipe for dark chocolate lovers. Note that the frosting needs to sit for at least two hours, so be sure to factor in enough time. Sometimes achieving the perfect texture is a bit difficult, but keep trying—if your frosting is too thick, simply whip in a bit more melted frosting; if it is too thin, whip in some more solid frosting. The results are worth the effort!

ENOUGH FROSTING FOR ONE 9-INCH THREE-LAYER CAKE

> 1 cup palm oil or coconut oil
>
> 4 cups (32 ounces) dairy-free dark chocolate chips
>
> 1 cup water
>
> ½ teaspoon sea salt
>
> 1 tablespoon plus 1 teaspoon vanilla extract, or 2 tablespoons cognac

1. In a double boiler, or with a metal mixing bowl placed over a pot of simmering water, melt the palm oil and chocolate, stirring frequently. When the mixture is melted completely, whisk in the water and salt by hand.

2. Let the frosting cool slightly in the mixing bowl, about 30 minutes, and whisk in the vanilla by hand. Set aside for 2 hours to allow the frosting to set. If the frosting becomes too hard to work with, remove a few scoops and melt again in a double boiler. Reincorporate the melted frosting into the solid frosting until you achieve a spreadable texture.

3. Use right away, or store in an airtight container in the refrigerator for up to 1 week. When you are ready to use the frosting, warm it slightly in a double boiler, or with a metal mixing bowl placed over a pot of simmering water, and whip it again until it is fluffy.

German Maple Frosting

The shreds of coconut and chunks of pecans in this frosting give it an exciting texture. This frosting works great with the Maple Cake (page 86) or Dark Chocolate Cake (page 88).

ENOUGH FROSTING FOR ONE 9-INCH THREE-LAYER CAKE

2½ cups palm oil or coconut oil

1 cup **maple syrup**

1 teaspoon sea salt

1 tablespoon vanilla extract

3½ cups shredded toasted coconut

1⅓ cups chopped toasted pecans

1. In the bowl of a standing mixer fitted with the paddle attachment, combine the palm oil, maple syrup, salt, and vanilla. Mix on low speed, gradually increasing the speed to high as the ingredients become incorporated. Add the coconut and pecans and beat until the frosting is fluffy.

2. Use right away, or store in an airtight container in the refrigerator for up to 1 week. When you are ready to use the frosting, warm it slightly in a double boiler, or with a metal mixing bowl placed over a pot of simmering water, and whip it again until it is fluffy.

Chai "Buttercream" Frosting

This unique frosting earns a lot of compliments from our customers. The deep, spicy tones of chai combine with the pure, smooth sweetness of the frosting to create something truly special.

ENOUGH FROSTING FOR ONE 9-INCH THREE-LAYER CAKE

  2 cups palm oil

  6⅔ cups **powdered organic whole cane sugar**, sifted

  ¼ teaspoon sea salt

  1 tablespoon ground cardamom

  1 tablespoon plus 1 teaspoon ground cloves

  ¾ cup hot, strongly steeped chai tea

  1 tablespoon plus 1 teaspoon vanilla extract

1. In the bowl of a standing mixer fitted with the paddle attachment, beat the palm oil and powdered organic whole cane sugar until soft. With the mixer on medium speed, add the salt, cardamom, cloves, chai tea, and vanilla. Continue to beat, scraping the sides of the bowl occasionally, until smooth and fluffy. To achieve the desired consistency, turn the mixer to high speed for 2 to 3 minutes.

2. Use right away, or store in an airtight container in the refrigerator for up to 1 week. When you are ready to use the frosting, warm it slightly in a double boiler, or with a metal mixing bowl placed over a pot of simmering water, and whip it again until it is fluffy.

Coconut Heaven Frosting

This blissful frosting will satisfy your coconut craving. Pair it with our Coconut Heaven Cake (page 87) for an extreme coconut experience.

ENOUGH FROSTING FOR ONE 9-INCH THREE-LAYER CAKE

> 3 cups palm oil or coconut oil
>
> 1½ cups **agave syrup** or **concentrated fruit juice** (I recommend Mystic Lake Dairy's pineapple-peach-pear juice concentrate)
>
> ⅛ teaspoon sea salt
>
> 1½ tablespoons vanilla extract
>
> 4½ cups shredded toasted coconut

1. In the bowl of a standing mixer fitted with the paddle attachment, combine the palm oil, agave syrup, salt, and vanilla. Mix on low speed, gradually increasing the speed to high as the ingredients become incorporated. Add the coconut and beat until the frosting is fluffy.

2. Use right away, or store in an airtight container in the refrigerator for up to 1 week. When you are ready to use the frosting, warm it slightly in a double boiler, or with a metal mixing bowl placed over a pot of simmering water, and whip it again until it is fluffy.

Agave-Sweetened Lemon Frosting

This creamy, zesty lemon frosting is bursting with flavor and will highlight even the most simple of cakes. Agave nectar has a very unique, natural taste that you'll feel good about eating.

ENOUGH FROSTING FOR ONE 9-INCH THREE-LAYER CAKE

> 3 cups palm oil or coconut oil
>
> 1½ cups **agave syrup**
>
> ⅛ teaspoon sea salt
>
> 1 tablespoon vanilla extract
>
> ½ teaspoon lemon oil
>
> Zest of one lemon

1. In the bowl of a standing mixer fitted with the paddle attachment, combine the palm oil, agave syrup, salt, vanilla, lemon oil, and lemon zest. Mix on low speed, gradually increasing the speed to high as the ingredients become incorporated. Beat until the frosting is fluffy.

2. Use right away, or store in an airtight container in the refrigerator for up to 1 week. When you are ready to use the frosting, warm it slightly in a double boiler, or with a metal mixing bowl placed over a pot of simmering water, and whip it again until it is fluffy.

Nut Butter Frosting

Jennifer Brown, one of the lovely bakers at Flying Apron, created this frosting to use in her Peanut Butter and Jelly Cake. I like to use almond butter, but feel free to experiment with any kind of nut butter. To make Peanut Butter and Jelly Cake, frost a Dark Chocolate Cake (page 88) with this frosting and strawberry preserves.

ENOUGH FROSTING FOR ONE 9-INCH THREE-LAYER CAKE

2 cups palm oil

6⅔ cups **powdered organic whole cane sugar**, sifted

½ teaspoon sea salt

2 tablespoons vanilla extract

1 cup nut butter

¾ cup boiling water

1. In the bowl of a standing mixer fitted with the paddle attachment, beat the palm oil and powdered organic whole cane sugar until soft. With the mixer on low speed, add the salt, vanilla, and nut butter. Continue to beat, scraping the sides of the bowl occasionally. Once the ingredients are incorporated, slowly add the boiling water, continuing to mix on high speed, until the frosting is smooth and fluffy.

2. Use right away, or store in an airtight container in the refrigerator for up to 1 week. When you are ready to use the frosting, warm it slightly in a double boiler, or with a metal mixing bowl placed over a pot of simmering water, and whip it again until it is fluffy.

Rose Tea–Infused Frosting

The delicate undertones of rose in this frosting add a sophisticated and romantic note to your dessert. Try pairing this frosting with Dark Chocolate Cake (page 88) or Maple Cake (page 86).

ENOUGH FROSTING FOR ONE 9-INCH THREE-LAYER CAKE

> 2 cups palm oil
>
> 6⅔ cups **powdered organic whole cane sugar**, sifted
>
> ½ teaspoon sea salt
>
> 1 cup hot, strongly steeped rose tea
>
> 2 tablespoons vanilla extract

1. In the bowl of a standing mixer fitted with the paddle attachment, beat the palm oil and powdered organic whole cane sugar until soft. With the mixer on low speed, add the salt, rose tea, and vanilla. Continue to beat, scraping the sides of the bowl occasionally, until smooth and fluffy. To achieve the desired consistency, turn the mixer to high speed for 2 to 3 minutes.

2. Use right away, or store in an airtight container in the refrigerator for up to 1 week. When you are ready to use the frosting, warm it slightly in a double boiler, or with a metal mixing bowl placed over a pot of simmering water, and whip it again until it is fluffy.

Chapter 6

BREADS

Inspired by an old-world staple, Flying Apron breads are unique. I think you will find these recipes delicious; they meet all of our needs like traditional breads while using predominantly wholesome flours and no refined starches. Because the ingredients are different from those in traditional breads, the techniques required to make them are, too. Children really love our Flying Apron Bakery House Bread (page 108), the Sweet Potato Rosemary Bread (page 111), and the Cinnamon Raisin Pecan Bread (page 113). The Dark Teff Grain Bread (page 115), Quinoa Bread (page 117), and Buckwheat Seed Bread (page 119) are likewise adored, particularly by those looking for a heartier, full-flavored bread. I hope you take great pleasure in the sensory experience of making nutritious, homemade bread.

Breads

Flying Apron Bakery House Bread (with Pizza Dough
and Individual Flatbreads variations)
Sweet Potato Rosemary Bread
Cinnamon Raisin Pecan Bread
Dark Teff Grain Bread
Quinoa Bread
Buckwheat Seed Bread

Essential Bread-Making Techniques

Because Flying Apron gluten-free breads are made with unrefined flours and do not include starch binders such as tapioca or potato, you will find that it is important to not overmix or overknead your dough. As soon as the loaves are shaped, the dough must go directly into the hot oven. The goal is to capture the gases of the yeast as the bread bakes rather than as the bread rises outside of the oven. As the yeast is activated, the gases that are released create small air pockets in the bread, giving it the light texture that is found in traditional wheat bread. Because we want to take advantage of the yeast gases expanding as the bread bakes, the temperature of the water used to activate the yeast is actually lukewarm, cooler than that of traditional wheat bread recipes. For traditional breads, gluten plays a key role in holding these pockets of air; with gluten-free bread it is a bit trickier: the bread must be baked simultaneously as the yeast is activating.

Flying Apron Bakery House Bread

This bread has a wonderful texture and mellow flavor that makes it perfect for sandwiches or toasting.

I LOAF

 2¾ cups brown rice flour

 1 cup garbanzo bean flour

 ¼ cup flax meal

 1½ teaspoons sea salt

 ¾ teaspoon xanthan gum

 ¼ cup extra-virgin olive oil

 ¼ cup **maple syrup**

 1 cup lukewarm water (94 degrees F)

 ½ tablespoon active dry yeast

 ⅓ cup pureed yam, sweet potato, or pumpkin

1. Preheat the oven to 300 degrees F. Lightly oil a baking pan or pizza stone. Dust your work surface liberally with brown rice flour.

2. Combine the brown rice flour, garbanzo bean flour, flax meal, salt, and xanthan gum in a large bowl. In the bowl of a standing mixer fitted with the paddle attachment, combine the olive oil, maple syrup, water, and yeast. As soon as the yeast is activated (the mixture will look cloudy and bubbles should form on the surface—it will take 3 to 5 minutes), turn the mixer on low speed. Add the flour mixture and yam alternately, a little at a time, until just incorporated, being careful not to overmix. (Alternatively, you can mix the dough by hand. Simply add the flour mixture and yam alternately to the oil mixture and mix until just incorporated.)

3. Once the ingredients are all incorporated, remove the dough from the bowl and quickly and gently knead it three or four times on your floured work surface. Shape the dough into a 12-inch-long loaf.

4. Moving quickly, place the loaf on the prepared baking pan or pizza stone. Lightly slash the loaf along the length of the side; this will allow excess air to escape so that the bread does not crack.

5. Bake until a knife inserted deep into the center comes out clean, about 2 hours and 5 minutes. Let the loaf cool for about 30 minutes before eating.

Pizza Dough

ONE 12-INCH PIZZA

1. Preheat the oven to 425 degrees F. Dust your work surface and rolling pin liberally with cornmeal. After kneading the dough a bit to form it into a ball, roll it out thinly and brush it with olive oil.

2. After adding your toppings, bake the pizza on a lightly oiled pizza stone or large baking sheet until the edges of the crust are firm and golden brown, about 15 minutes.

Individual Flatbreads

8 TO 10 FLATBREADS

1. Preheat the oven to 375 degrees F. Dust your work surface and rolling pin liberally with brown rice flour. After kneading the dough, divide it into 8 to 10 portions. Roll out the individual pieces of dough to ½ inch thick and transfer to 2 lightly oiled baking sheets (reuse as needed).

2. Brush each flatbread liberally with olive oil and sprinkle with fresh or dried herbs. (Rosemary and coarse sea salt is a winning combination. Za'atar spice mix or curry powder and sea salt are also delicious.)

3. Bake until the flatbread is light brown and slightly firm, 15 to 20 minutes.

Sweet Potato Rosemary Bread

A Thanksgiving tradition at the Flying Apron, these nourishing breads and rolls are extremely popular. The sweet potato's gorgeous earthy color and rosemary's pungent aroma excite the senses.

I LOAF

    3½ cups brown rice flour

    1 cup garbanzo bean flour

    ¼ cup flax meal

    ½ tablespoon dried rosemary

    ¾ teaspoon sea salt

    ¾ teaspoon xanthan gum

    ¼ cup extra-virgin olive oil

    ¼ cup **maple syrup**

    1 cup lukewarm water (94 degrees F)

    ½ tablespoon cake yeast

    1 cup pureed sweet potato or yam

1. Preheat the oven to 300 degrees F. Lightly oil a baking pan or pizza stone. Dust your work surface liberally with brown rice flour.

2. Combine the brown rice flour, garbanzo bean flour, flax meal, rosemary, salt, and xanthan gum in a large bowl. In the bowl of a standing mixer fitted with a dough hook, combine the olive oil, maple syrup, water, and yeast. As soon as the yeast is activated (the mixture will look cloudy and bubbles should form on the surface—it will take 3 to 5 minutes), turn the mixer on low speed. Add the flour mixture and sweet potato alternately, a little at a time, until just incorporated, being careful not to overmix. (Alternatively, you can mix the dough by hand. Simply add the flour mixture and sweet potato alternately to the oil mixture and mix until just incorporated.)

3. Once the ingredients are all incorporated, remove the dough from the bowl and quickly and gently knead it three or four times on your floured surface. Shape the dough into a 12-inch-long loaf.

4. Moving quickly, place the loaf on the prepared baking pan or pizza stone. Lightly slash the loaf along the length of the top; this will allow excess air to escape so that the bread does not crack.

5. Bake until a knife inserted deep into the center of the loaf comes out clean, about 2 hours and 5 minutes.

Cinnamon Raisin Pecan Bread

This slightly sweet, hearty bread is delightful. Enjoy a toasted slice in the morning with your tea.

I LOAF

    1 cup teff flour

    ¾ cup brown rice flour

    1 cup garbanzo bean flour

    ¼ cup flax meal

    ½ cup raisins

    ½ cup chopped pecans

    ¾ teaspoon ground cinnamon

    ¾ teaspoon sea salt

    ¾ teaspoon xanthan gum

    ¼ cup extra-virgin olive oil

    ¼ cup **maple syrup**

    1 cup lukewarm water (94 degrees F)

    ½ tablespoon cake yeast

    ⅓ cup pureed yam, sweet potato, or pumpkin

1. Preheat the oven to 300 degrees F. Lightly oil a baking pan or pizza stone. Dust your work surface liberally with brown rice flour.

2. Combine the teff flour, brown rice flour, garbanzo bean flour, flax meal, raisins, pecans, cinnamon, salt, and xanthan gum in a large bowl. In the bowl of a standing mixer fitted with a dough hook, combine the olive oil, maple syrup, water, and yeast. As soon as the yeast is activated (the mixture will look cloudy and bubbles should form on the surface—it will take 3 to 5 minutes), turn the mixer on low speed. Add the flour mixture and yam alternately, a little at a time, until just incorporated, being careful not to overmix. (Alternatively, you can mix the dough by hand. Simply add the flour mixture and yam alternately to the oil mixture and mix until just incorporated.)

3. Once the ingredients are all incorporated, remove the dough from the bowl and quickly and gently knead it three or four times on your floured work surface. Shape the dough into a 12-inch-long loaf.

4. Moving quickly, place the loaf on the prepared baking pan or pizza stone. Lightly slash the loaf along the length of the side; this will allow excess air to escape so that the bread does not crack.

5. Bake until a knife inserted deep into the center of the loaf comes out clean, about 2 hours and 5 minutes.

Dark Teff Grain Bread

Teff is an ancient Ethiopian grain that is celebrated for its remarkable nutritional value, especially for its protein, fiber, and iron content. This is a healthy and mouthwatering staple that you really need to try.

1 LOAF

      2¾ cups teff flour

      1 cup garbanzo bean flour

      ¼ cup flax meal

      ¾ teaspoon sea salt

      ¾ teaspoon xanthan gum

      ¼ cup extra-virgin olive oil

      ¼ cup **maple syrup**

      1 cup lukewarm water (94 degrees F)

      ½ tablespoon cake yeast

      ⅓ cup pureed yam, sweet potato, or pumpkin

1. Preheat the oven to 300 degrees F. Lightly oil a baking pan or pizza stone. Dust your work surface liberally with brown rice flour.

2. Combine the teff flour, garbanzo bean flour, flax meal, salt, and xanthan gum in a large bowl. In the bowl of a standing mixer fitted with the paddle attachment, combine the olive oil, maple syrup, water, and yeast. As soon as the yeast is activated (the mixture will look cloudy and bubbles should form on the surface—it will take 3 to 5 minutes), turn the mixer on low speed. Add the flour mixture and yam alternately, a little at a time, until just incorporated, being careful not to overmix. (Alternatively, you can mix the dough by hand. Simply add the flour mixture and yam alternately to the oil mixture and mix until just incorporated.)

3. Once the ingredients are all incorporated, remove the dough from the bowl and quickly and gently knead it three or four times on your floured work surface. Shape the dough into a 12-inch-long loaf.

4. Moving quickly, place the loaf on the prepared baking pan or pizza stone. Lightly slash the loaf along the length of the side; this will allow excess air to escape so that the bread does not crack.

5. Bake until a knife inserted deep into the center of the loaf comes out clean, about 2 hours and 5 minutes.

Quinoa Bread

Many of our customers at Flying Apron are die-hard fans of this bread. Do be aware, though, that adults tend to appreciate its unique flavor more than children do. This bread also makes for a delicious high-protein pizza crust. Simply make your dough and follow the baking instructions for Pizza Dough on page 110. As quinoa flour is a little pricey, using brown rice flour or cornmeal on your working surface might be a more economical option.

I LOAF

> 1¾ cups quinoa flour
>
> ¼ teaspoon baking soda
>
> ¾ teaspoon sea salt, plus more for sprinkling on top of the bread
>
> 2 tablespoons extra-virgin olive oil
>
> 2 tablespoons **brown rice syrup**
>
> ½ cup plus 2 tablespoons water

1. Preheat the oven to 300 degrees F. Lightly oil a baking pan or pizza stone. Dust your work surface liberally with quinoa flour.

2. Combine the quinoa flour, baking soda, salt, olive oil, brown rice syrup, and water in the bowl of a standing mixer fitted with the paddle attachment. Mix on low speed until well incorporated.

3. Once the ingredients are all incorporated, remove the dough from the bowl and place it on your floured work surface. Shape the dough into a 12-inch-long loaf.

4. Moving quickly, place the loaf on the prepared baking pan or pizza stone. Sprinkle the top with salt and lightly slash the loaf along the length of the side; this will allow excess air to escape so that the bread does not crack.

5. Bake until a knife inserted deep into the center of the loaf comes out clean, about 1 hour and 30 minutes. Let the loaf cool for about 30 minutes before eating.

Buckwheat Seed Bread

This bread is chock-full of seeds and grains that make it satisfying and robust. I like to decorate the top of the bread with poppy seeds, but any seeds will do.

I LOAF

> 1⅔ cups brown rice flour
>
> 2 cups buckwheat flour
>
> 1 cup corn flour
>
> 1¼ cups cornmeal
>
> 2 teaspoons baking powder
>
> 2 teaspoons baking soda
>
> 1½ teaspoons sea salt
>
> ¾ cup raw unsalted pumpkin seeds
>
> ½ cup raw unsalted sunflower seeds
>
> 1 tablespoon flax seeds
>
> 5½ cups water
>
> 2 tablespoons **molasses**
>
> Seeds for sprinkling on top of the bread

1. Preheat the oven to 350 degrees F. Lightly oil a 9⅞- by 3⅛-inch bread pan and line with parchment paper.

2. Combine the brown rice flour, buckwheat flour, corn flour, cornmeal, baking powder, baking soda, salt, pumpkin seeds, sunflower seeds, flax seeds, water, and molasses in the bowl of a standing mixer fitted with the paddle attachment. Mix on low speed until well incorporated.

3. Pour the batter into the prepared bread pan, filling three quarters of the way full. Sprinkle the top with seeds and bake until a knife inserted deep into the center of the loaf comes out clean, about 1 hour and 40 minutes.

Chapter 7

SAVORY FARE

Having the expansive space in our Fremont location has really allowed us to explore the savory side of life! We began making miniature pizzas and flatbreads early on in the bakery's history and have truly enjoyed expanding in this area ever since. Offering savory fare has made for such a well-rounded experience for our customers—now they are able to stop in and enjoy a complete, nutritious meal. The additional smells of hearty soups simmering, vegetables roasting, and spices toasting, combined with the aromas of cakes baking and chocolate melting, have created a delightful and inspiring atmosphere for all.

Hearty Entrées

Indian Curry Apron Pockets

Russian Potato and Cabbage Piroshki

Italian Mushroom Apron Pockets

Pizza Verdura

Polenta Cannellini Bean Torte with Caponata

Gnocchi with Herbed Pistou

Soups

Lentil Dahl

Italian White Bean and Tomato Soup

Simple Carrot Fennel Soup

Borscht

Sorrel, Leek, and Potato Soup

Spring Pea Soup with Cashew Cream and Dill

Salads

Roasted Beets with Rosemary

White Bean and Butternut Squash Provençal

Quinoa with Sautéed Leeks and Chanterelles

Millet with Basil Pesto, Sun-Dried Tomatoes, and Pine Nuts

Buckwheat Soba Noodle Salad

Chinese Green Beans

Balsamic-Roasted Red Garnet Yams

Moroccan Bean Salad over Baby Spinach

Asian Kale

Hijiki Carrot Slaw

Cherry Tomatoes with Fresh Herbs and White Balsamic Vinegar

Sweet Golden Beets with Toasted Pecans and Currants

Pea Shoot, Chive, and Apricot Salad with Honey Mustard Dressing

Dinosaur Kale, Artichoke, and Garbanzo Bean Salad

Hearty Entrées

Here you will find recipes that will wow guests as the main focus at a fancy table, as well as entrées that are easy to pack for a picnic. The Indian Curry Apron Pockets (page 124) and Italian Mushroom Apron Pockets (page 129) are terrific choices for an outdoor affair, as they are portable and made in individual portions. The Gnocchi with Herbed Pistou (page 134) and Polenta Cannellini Bean Torte with Caponata (page 132), however, should be enjoyed as soon as they are ready; with their elegant appearance and delicious taste, they will make for a memorable evening.

Indian Curry Apron Pockets

This curried vegetable pocket is a great alternative to the souplike curries that many people are so fond of. The tasty vegetables and bite of curry go beautifully with the flaky-crust pocket.

8 TO 10 SERVINGS

> 2 tablespoons extra-virgin olive oil, plus more for brushing the pockets
>
> ½ teaspoon black mustard seeds
>
> 1 teaspoon cumin seeds
>
> 2 teaspoons curry powder, plus more for sprinkling the pockets
>
> ⅛ teaspoon cayenne
>
> 1 medium yellow onion, diced
>
> 2 cloves garlic, minced
>
> 1 medium sweet potato, peeled and cut into ½-inch dice
>
> 1 medium carrot, peeled, halved, and thinly sliced
>
> One 13.5-ounce can coconut milk
>
> 1½ cups broccoli florets
>
> 1 cup peas, fresh or frozen
>
> 1⅔ cups cooked garbanzo beans, or one 15-ounce can, drained
>
> Sea salt
>
> 1 batch *unbaked* Flying Apron Bakery House Bread (page 108)
>
> Brown rice flour, for rolling out dough

1. Heat the olive oil in a large sauté pan over medium heat. Add the mustard seeds, cumin seeds, curry powder, and cayenne. Cook, stirring constantly, until the mustard seeds begin to pop, about 3 minutes. Add the onion and garlic, and sauté until the onion begins to soften, about 5 minutes.

2. Add the sweet potato and carrot, tossing to coat with the spice mixture. Add the coconut milk and simmer, covered, until the vegetables are cooked through and soft, about 15 minutes. Add the broccoli and peas and simmer, covered, until the broccoli is tender, about 7 minutes. Add the garbanzo beans and salt to taste, then remove the pan from the heat and keep warm.

3. Preheat the oven to 350 degrees F.

4. Divide the bread dough into 8 to 10 pieces, depending on the number of portions you wish to make. Dust your counter liberally with brown rice flour and roll out each piece into approximately 7-inch circles. On one half of the circle, place approximately ½ cup of the filling. Fold the other half of the dough over the filling and seal the edges by crimping with your fingers or a fork.

5. Carefully transfer the pockets to a well-oiled baking sheet. Brush the tops with olive oil and sprinkle with curry powder and salt. Bake until the thickest part of the pocket is firm and beginning to brown, about 25 minutes.

Russian Potato and Cabbage Piroshki

This is a slightly more elaborate version of an old-world staple. These make a surprisingly substantial meal. Be sure to serve them right away—they taste best when they are piping hot.

8 TO 10 SERVINGS

  2 Yukon gold potatoes (about 1 pound), peeled and diced

  1 cup finely shredded green cabbage

  1 tablespoon extra-virgin olive oil, plus more for brushing the piroshkis

  1 medium yellow onion, diced

  ½ teaspoon caraway seeds

  ½ teaspoon dill seeds

  1⅔ cups cooked navy beans, or one 15-ounce can, drained

  1 tablespoon snipped fresh dill, plus more for sprinkling the piroshkis

  1 teaspoon sea salt

  1 batch *unbaked* Flying Apron Bakery House Bread (page 108)

  Brown rice flour, for rolling out dough

1. Cook the diced potatoes either by using a steamer basket or boiling them until tender, about 10 minutes. Add the cabbage and cook for another 4 to 5 minutes until the cabbage is tender. Set aside.

2. Heat the olive oil in a large skillet over medium heat. Add the onion and sauté until slightly brown, about 5 minutes. Add the caraway seeds, dill seeds, navy beans, fresh dill, salt, and the reserved potatoes and cabbage, and stir to combine.

3. Preheat the oven to 350 degrees F.

4. Divide the bread dough into 8 to 10 pieces, depending on the number of portions you wish to make. Dust your counter liberally with brown rice flour and roll out each piece into approximately 7-inch circles. On one half of the circle, place approximately ⅓ cup of the filling. Fold the other half of the dough over the filling and seal the edges by crimping with your fingers or a fork. At this point, the piroshkis can be baked, or they can be frozen in an airtight container for up to 2 weeks. When ready to use, thaw completely before baking.

5. Carefully transfer the piroshkis to a well-oiled baking sheet. Brush the tops with olive oil and sprinkle with fresh dill. Bake until the piroshkis are light golden brown, about 30 minutes. Serve immediately.

Italian Mushroom Apron Pockets

The distinctive taste of mushrooms is pleasantly highlighted by traditional Italian spices, making these pockets a really special treat. If you choose to make the Homemade Marinara Sauce recipe I've included, be sure to have it prepared beforehand.

8 TO 10 SERVINGS

1 tablespoon extra-virgin olive oil, plus more for brushing the pockets

1 medium yellow onion, quartered and thinly sliced

1 green bell pepper, seeded and diced

3 cloves garlic, minced

2 portobello mushrooms, sliced into 1-inch-thick strips

1 tablespoon finely chopped fresh basil

1 teaspoon dried oregano, plus more for sprinkling the pockets (optional)

½ teaspoon dried thyme, plus more for sprinkling the pockets (optional)

1 teaspoon dried rosemary, plus more for sprinkling the pockets (optional)

½ cup oil-packed sun-dried tomatoes, thinly sliced

1⅔ cups cooked navy beans, or one 15-ounce can, drained

4 cups loosely packed baby spinach

Sea salt and freshly ground pepper

1 batch *unbaked* Flying Apron Bakery House Bread (page 108)

Brown rice flour, for rolling out dough

Homemade Marinara Sauce (recipe follows) or your favorite jarred sauce

1. Heat the olive oil in a large sauté pan over medium heat. Add the onion and sauté until slightly brown, about 7 minutes. Add the bell pepper and garlic and sauté until the peppers are soft but not soggy, about 5 minutes. Add the mushrooms, basil, oregano, thyme, and rosemary and cook, stirring occasionally, until the mushrooms begin to release some of their juices, about 7 minutes. Add the sun-dried tomatoes and navy beans and stir to combine. Stir in the fresh spinach and season to taste with salt and pepper. Cook, stirring occasionally, until the mixture is hot, about 7 minutes.

2. Preheat the oven to 350 degrees F.

3. Divide the bread dough into 8 to 10 pieces, depending on the number of portions you wish to make. Dust your counter liberally with brown rice flour and roll out each piece into approximately 7-inch circles. Spread a spoonful of Homemade Marinara Sauce over the circle, leaving 1 inch around the perimeter of the dough. On one half of the circle, place approximately ½ cup of the filling. Fold the other half of the dough over the filling and seal the edges by crimping with your fingers or a fork.

4. Carefully transfer the pockets to a well-oiled baking sheet. Brush the tops with olive oil and sprinkle with additional herbs. Bake until the thickest part of the pocket is firm and beginning to brown, about 30 minutes.

Homemade Marinara Sauce

3½ CUPS SAUCE

> ¼ cup extra-virgin olive oil
>
> 2 shallots, chopped
>
> 3 cloves garlic, chopped
>
> One 35-ounce can whole peeled Italian tomatoes
>
> 2 tablespoons chopped fresh basil
>
> ¼ cup dry white wine
>
> Sea salt and freshly ground pepper

1. Heat the olive oil in a large saucepan over medium heat. Add the shallots and garlic and sauté until lightly brown, about 7 minutes. Add the tomatoes and basil, crushing the tomatoes with the back of a wooden spoon to break them into pieces. Add the white wine and bring to a boil. Turn the heat to low and simmer, uncovered, until thickened, 30 to 45 minutes. Season with salt and pepper.

Pizza Verdura

At Flying Apron, we stay busy every weekend by participating in our local farmers markets. One of our bestsellers is a mini version of this pizza. The hearty texture of the crust and beautiful fresh vegetables piled on top make it irresistible.

4 TO 6 SERVINGS

2 tablespoons extra-virgin olive oil, plus more for brushing the pizza dough

1 medium yellow onion, halved and thinly sliced

1 green bell pepper, seeded, quartered and thinly sliced

1 yellow bell pepper, seeded, quartered, and thinly sliced

6 medium tomatoes, diced

¼ cup dried porcini mushrooms, soaked in water for 25 minutes

1½ tablespoons white wine

½ cup kalamata olives, roughly chopped

4 cups loosely packed spinach

Sea salt and freshly ground pepper

1 batch *unbaked* Flying Apron Bakery House Bread (page 108)

Cornmeal, for rolling out dough

5 tablespoons finely chopped fresh basil

1. Heat the olive oil in a large sauté pan over medium heat. Add the onion and sauté until softened, about 7 minutes. Add the peppers and continue to cook until they soften, about 8 minutes. Add the tomatoes, mushrooms, and wine. Cook, stirring occasionally, for 12 minutes. Add the olives and spinach. Remove from heat. Add salt and pepper to taste.

2. Preheat the oven to 425 degrees F.

3. Dust your counter liberally with cornmeal. Roll out the dough to ½ inch thick and place it on a pizza stone. Brush the dough with olive oil and spread the vegetable mixture evenly over the dough. Sprinkle with the basil and bake until the crust is golden brown and the toppings are well cooked, about 15 minutes.

Polenta Cannellini Bean Torte with Caponata

This colorful torte is not only beautiful, but also delicious and nutritious. The layers of bright yellow polenta contrasted with the greens and beans will entice you and your guests—and don't forget a generous serving of Caponata on the side! I suggest making the Caponata first so that the flavors have time to meld while you prepare the torte.

4 TO 6 SERVINGS

2 tablespoons extra-virgin olive oil

1 medium yellow onion, quartered and thinly sliced

1 teaspoon dried sage

1½ teaspoons sea salt, divided

1⅔ cups cooked cannellini beans, or one 15-ounce can, drained

3 cups water

1 cup polenta

½ teaspoon dried oregano

4 cups loosely packed spinach

Freshly ground pepper

Caponata (recipe follows)

1. Heat the olive oil in a large sauté pan over medium heat. Add the onion and sauté until it begins to soften and caramelize, about 7 minutes. Add the sage, 1 teaspoon of the salt, and the beans. Lower the heat and simmer.

2. Meanwhile, bring the water to a boil with the remaining ½ teaspoon salt. Slowly add the polenta and oregano, stirring constantly. Once you have added all of the polenta, turn the heat to low and simmer, stirring constantly, until the polenta becomes thick, 15 to 30 minutes, depending on the coarseness of your polenta.

3. Preheat the oven to 350 degrees F.

4. Lightly oil a 9-inch springform pan.

5. Add the spinach to the simmering beans and stir just until it is wilted. Season with pepper. Remove the sauté pan from the heat.

6. Spread half of the polenta over the bottom of the springform pan. Add the bean mixture and spread evenly. Spread the second half of the polenta over the top. Brush with olive oil and sprinkle with salt and pepper. Bake until the polenta is firm, about 25 minutes.

7. Carefully remove the torte from the pan and transfer it to a serving plate. Cut into wedges and top each wedge generously with Caponata.

Caponata

3 CUPS CAPONATA

>   1 medium eggplant (about 1 pound), cut into 1-inch cubes
>
>   10 cloves garlic, peeled
>
>   ¼ cup extra-virgin olive oil
>
>   1 teaspoon sea salt
>
>   One 15-ounce can diced tomatoes, drained
>
>   2 tablespoons balsamic vinegar
>
>   ¾ cup kalamata olives, roughly chopped
>
>   2 tablespoons chopped Italian parsley, for garnish

1. Preheat the oven to 410 degrees F.

2. Place the eggplant, garlic, olive oil, and salt in a glass baking dish. Toss to coat. Bake until the eggplant is soft, about 30 minutes.

3. Stir in the tomatoes, balsamic vinegar, and olives. Transfer to a serving dish. Just before serving, garnish with the parsley.

Gnocchi with Herbed Pistou

This version of the classic Italian dish retains all the richness of the original. And the simple, yet vibrant, flavors of the pistou only add to its goodness. If you prefer, the gnocchi are also good with Homemade Marinara Sauce (page 130). I recommend that when you make this dish, you first form the gnocchi, then make the Herbed Pistou (or Homemade Marinara Sauce), and then cook the gnocchi. Dress the gnocchi with as much or as little of the Herbed Pistou as you like. Any leftover sauce makes an amazing bread dip and also serves well as a dressing for vegetables.

4 TO 6 SERVINGS

> 3 medium Yukon gold potatoes (about 2 pounds)
>
> 2 tablespoons extra-virgin olive oil
>
> ½ teaspoon sea salt
>
> ⅛ teaspoon nutmeg
>
> 1¼ cups buckwheat flour
>
> ⅓ cup water
>
> Brown rice flour, for rolling out dough
>
> Herbed Pistou (recipe follows)
>
> 8 sprigs thyme, for garnish

1. Bring a large pot of lightly salted water to a boil. Add the potatoes, reduce the heat to low, and simmer the potatoes until they are soft, about 45 minutes.

2. When the potatoes are done cooking, place them directly into a bath of cold water. Once they are cool, remove and peel them. Place the peeled potatoes in a large bowl and mash them with a potato masher or a fork, or push them through a potato ricer. Add the olive oil, salt, and nutmeg. Mix well.

3. Gradually add the buckwheat flour to the potato mixture. Once it is incorporated, add the water and knead the dough with your hands until it is fully combined, about 5 minutes.

4. Divide the dough into 6 portions. Dust your work surface and rolling pin liberally with brown rice flour. Roll each portion into a ½-inch-thick rope. Slice into 1-inch pieces. Press a floured fork gently into each gnocchi to create a light impression. Transfer the gnocchi to a floured plate.

5. Preheat the oven to 200 degrees F. Place an oiled baking sheet in the oven.

6. Bring a shallow pot of salted water to a boil with your steamer basket in place. The water level should be lower than the steamer basket to ensure the water does not touch the gnocchi. Working in batches, steam the gnocchi until just firm, about 7 minutes. Remove from the steamer basket carefully with a slotted spoon or spatula. Transfer the cooked gnocchi to the baking sheet in the oven to keep warm until all the gnocchi are cooked.

7. Serve drizzled liberally with Herbed Pistou and garnished with fresh thyme.

Herbed Pistou

2½ CUPS PISTOU

> ¾ cup fresh basil
>
> ½ cup Italian parsley
>
> 2 tablespoons fresh thyme
>
> 1 tablespoon fresh rosemary
>
> 1 tablespoon fresh oregano
>
> 2 cloves garlic, peeled
>
> 1 cup extra-virgin olive oil
>
> ⅛ teaspoon red pepper flakes
>
> Sea salt and freshly ground pepper

1. Combine the basil, parsley, thyme, rosemary, oregano, and garlic in a food processor. With the motor running, gradually add the olive oil and red pepper flakes. Add salt and pepper to taste.

Soups

Soups are so healing, comforting, and easy to make. And I love leftover soup—it makes for a quick lunch fix! The flavors of the soup often intensify overnight, making it even more delicious the next day. The following soups vary in consistency from thick and creamy to light with lots of vegetables.

Lentil Dahl

At Flying Apron, this soup is always snatched up quickly, especially on cold days. Its thick consistency and lentils' high protein content make this soup a meal in itself.

6 TO 8 SERVINGS

6 cups vegetable stock

1½ cups yellow split peas

1 medium yellow onion, diced

1 medium sweet potato, peeled and diced

1 medium Yukon gold potato, peeled and cut into ½-inch dice

1 medium carrot, peeled and thinly sliced

2 cloves garlic, minced

One 14.5-ounce can diced tomatoes

2 tablespoons extra-virgin olive oil

1½ teaspoons black mustard seeds

3 teaspoons cumin seeds

2 teaspoons dried coriander

2 teaspoons curry powder

1 teaspoon turmeric

⅛ teaspoon cayenne

1 teaspoon grated fresh gingerroot

Sea salt

Lemon wedges, for garnish

1. In a large soup pot, bring the vegetable stock and split peas to a boil. Reduce the heat and simmer, covered, until the peas are tender, about 30 minutes.

2. Add the onion, sweet potato, Yukon gold potato, carrot, garlic, and tomatoes. Return to a boil. Reduce the heat and simmer, covered, until the potatoes are tender, about 15 minutes.

3. While the soup is simmering, heat the olive oil in a small sauté pan over medium heat. Add the mustard seeds, cumin seeds, coriander, curry powder, turmeric, cayenne, and gingerroot. Cook, stirring, just until the seeds begin to pop, about 3 minutes.

4. Stir the spice mixture into the soup and add salt to taste. Serve with the lemon wedges on the side.

Italian White Bean and Tomato Soup

This soup, with its deep flavor, tastes like it's been cooking all day. However, it comes together in under an hour. I really enjoy the creaminess of the white beans.

6 TO 8 SERVINGS

    1 tablespoon extra-virgin olive oil

    1 medium yellow onion, diced

    2 celery ribs, finely chopped

    1 medium carrot, peeled and finely chopped

    5 medium tomatoes, diced

    ½ cup dry white wine

    3 cups water

    1 bay leaf

    2 teaspoons chopped fresh oregano

    3 cups cooked cannellini or navy beans, or two 15-ounce cans, drained

    Sea salt and freshly ground pepper

1. Heat the olive oil in a large soup pot over medium heat. Add the onion and sauté until lightly brown, about 7 minutes. Add the celery, carrot, and tomatoes and sauté for an additional 5 minutes. Add the white wine and cook until reduced slightly, about 5 minutes. Add the water, bay leaf, oregano, and cannellini beans, and bring to a boil. Reduce the heat to low and simmer, covered, for 30 minutes.

2. Remove half of the soup from the pot and puree it in a blender, being very careful not to splash the soup. Return the pureed soup to the pot and add salt and pepper to taste.

Simple Carrot Fennel Soup

This soup comes together quickly and is mellow and smooth in flavor. The rich carrot flavor pairs nicely with a kale salad.

6 SERVINGS

½ teaspoon fennel seeds

1 tablespoon extra-virgin olive oil

1 medium yellow onion, finely diced

1 fennel bulb, halved and thinly sliced, fronds reserved for garnish

4 cups vegetable stock

1½ pounds carrots (about 14 small carrots), cut into ½-inch rounds

2 teaspoons sea salt

One 14-ounce can coconut milk

Freshly ground pepper

1. In a small skillet over medium heat, toast the fennel seeds until they are aromatic, about 4 minutes. Crush them with a mortar and pestle, or on a cutting board using a rolling pin, and set aside.

2. Heat the olive oil in a large soup pot over medium heat. Add the onion and sauté until softened, about 5 minutes. Add the fennel and continue to sauté for another 5 minutes. Add the vegetable stock, carrots, salt, and reserved fennel seeds, and bring to a boil. Reduce the heat to low and simmer, covered, until the carrots are very soft, about 30 minutes.

3. Remove the soup from the stove and puree with an immersion blender or in batches in a blender, being very careful not to splash the soup. Return to the pot and stir in the coconut milk. Add pepper to taste. Serve in individual bowls, garnished with fennel fronds.

Borscht

This soup is rich in nutrients and very sustaining. For a Russian-inspired evening, serve this soup with the Russian Potato and Cabbage Piroshki (page 126). The Cashew Cream offers a cool, smooth contrast to the hot, hearty soup.

8 SERVINGS

> 1 tablespoon extra-virgin olive oil
>
> 1 medium yellow onion, diced
>
> 6 beets, peeled, halved, and julienned
>
> 1 large carrot, peeled and julienned
>
> 1 medium yam, peeled and julienned
>
> 6 cups vegetable stock
>
> 2 medium tomatoes, diced
>
> Juice of 1 lemon
>
> 1 tablespoon snipped fresh dill, plus additional dill sprigs for garnish
>
> ½ teaspoon dill seed
>
> 2 teaspoons sea salt
>
> 3 cups shredded green cabbage
>
> Cashew Cream (recipe follows)

1. Heat the olive oil in a large soup pot over medium heat. Add the onion and sauté until transparent and softened, about 5 minutes. Add the beets, carrot, and yam, and briefly sauté. Add the vegetable stock and bring to a boil. Add the tomatoes, lemon juice, dill, dill seed, and salt. Reduce the heat to low and simmer, covered, for 35 minutes.

2. Add the cabbage and simmer just until it is tender, about 5 minutes.

3. Ladle the soup into individual serving bowls, drizzle with Cashew Cream, and garnish with fresh dill sprigs.

Cashew Cream

     1 cup cashews, soaked for 2 hours in water and then drained

     Juice of 1 lemon

     1 tablespoon snipped fresh dill

     1 teaspoon sea salt

     ¼ cup water

1. Combine the cashews, lemon juice, dill, salt, and water in a food processor and blend until creamy. Store any unused cream in an airtight container in the refrigerator for up to 1 week.

Sorrel, Leek, and Potato Soup

This is a thick and velvety soup. The abundance of spinach gives the soup a lovely green color. When sorrel isn't in season, a quarter cup of fresh tarragon substitutes nicely, with an additional three-quarters cup of fresh spinach.

6 TO 8 SERVINGS

1 tablespoon extra-virgin olive oil

2 leeks, halved, thinly sliced, and washed (about 1½ cups)

4 medium Yukon gold potatoes (about 2 pounds), cut into ¼-inch dice

5 cups vegetable stock

1 cup chopped fresh sorrel

8 cups loosely packed spinach

2 teaspoons sea salt

¼ teaspoon white pepper

Lemon wedges, for garnish

1. Heat the olive oil in a large soup pot over medium heat. Add the leeks and sauté until softened and lightly browned, about 5 minutes. Add the potatoes and stir to coat. Add the vegetable stock and bring to a boil. Reduce the heat to low and simmer, covered, until the potatoes are soft, about 30 minutes. Add the sorrel, spinach, salt, and white pepper. Stir until the greens are just wilted, about 1 minute.

2. Remove the soup from the stove and puree with an immersion blender or in batches in a blender, being very careful not to splash the soup. Return to the pot and add more salt and pepper to taste. Serve with lemon wedges on the side.

Spring Pea Soup with Cashew Cream and Dill

This is a refreshing and simple soup. Pair it with miniature tea sandwiches for a sophisticated lunch party.

4 TO 6 SERVINGS

    2 tablespoons extra-virgin olive oil

    6 shallots, finely chopped

    4 cups water

    1 teaspoon sea salt

    6 cups peas, fresh or frozen

    2 tablespoons snipped fresh dill, plus additional for garnish

    Freshly ground pepper

    Cashew Cream (page 144)

1. Heat the olive oil in a large soup pot over medium heat. Add the shallots and sauté until just beginning to brown, about 5 minutes. Add the water, salt, and peas. Reduce the heat to low and simmer, covered, until the peas are soft, about 15 minutes. Stir in the dill.

2. Remove the soup from the stove and puree with an immersion blender or in batches in a blender, being very careful not to splash the soup. Return to the pot and add pepper to taste and more salt, if needed. Serve in individual bowls, drizzled with Cashew Cream and garnished with dill.

Salads

Warm salads are particularly nice to have on cool evenings. The warm salads included here are also delicious when served at room temperature, which makes them fantastic picnic fare.

All of the cool salads are full of high-quality, healthy ingredients. I recommend choosing a salad based on which ingredients are in season—for example, I look forward to spring every year so that I can make the Pea Shoot, Chive, and Apricot Salad with Honey Mustard Dressing (page 162). Eating lots of vegetables is easy when they are in season and dressed with flavorful oils, vinegars, and herbs.

Roasted Beets with Rosemary

The ingredients for this salad are few and simple, but don't be fooled—this unpretentious and rustic dish is a real winner and makes a great addition to any Italian-themed meal.

4 TO 6 SERVINGS

> 6 beets, peeled, halved, and thinly sliced, greens reserved and torn into bite-sized pieces
>
> ¼ cup extra-virgin olive oil
>
> 1 teaspoon sea salt
>
> 1 tablespoon dried rosemary
>
> 12 cloves garlic, peeled and halved
>
> Juice of ½ lemon
>
> Freshly ground pepper

1. Preheat the oven to 425 degrees F.

2. In a large glass baking dish, combine the beets, olive oil, salt, rosemary, and garlic. Toss to coat the beets well and bake until tender, about 40 minutes. Add the reserved beet greens, toss well, and bake for an additional 5 minutes.

3. Remove from the oven and add lemon juice and pepper to taste. Transfer to a serving platter and enjoy.

White Bean and Butternut Squash Provençal

Although this dish is very easy to make, it's so good that people will think you spent hours in the kitchen.

4 TO 6 SERVINGS

> 1 medium butternut squash (2 pounds), peeled and cut into 1-inch cubes
>
> 1 medium yellow onion, quartered and thinly sliced
>
> 2 tablespoons extra-virgin olive oil
>
> 2 teaspoons sea salt
>
> 1 teaspoon dried oregano, plus additional for garnish
>
> 1 teaspoon dried thyme, plus additional for garnish
>
> 1 teaspoon dried rosemary
>
> ½ cup dry white wine
>
> 1⅔ cups cooked navy beans, or one 15-ounce can, drained

1. Preheat the oven to 400 degrees F.

2. In a roasting pan or large glass baking dish, combine the squash, onion, olive oil, salt, oregano, thyme, and rosemary. Drizzle with the wine and bake until the squash is cooked through and tender, about 30 minutes. Add the beans and toss to combine. Transfer to a serving platter and garnish with oregano and thyme.

Quinoa with Sautéed Leeks and Chanterelles

Chanterelle mushrooms are known for their mild peppery taste and firm, meaty texture. Combining them with savory leeks and quinoa makes for a beautiful dish.

4 TO 6 SERVINGS

   2 cups vegetable stock

   1 cup quinoa, rinsed

   1 teaspoon sea salt, divided

   2 tablespoons extra-virgin olive oil

   2 leeks, halved, thinly sliced, and washed

   2 cups sliced chanterelle mushrooms

   2 cups sliced cremini mushrooms

   1 tablespoon chopped fresh lemon thyme, plus additional sprigs for garnish

   Freshly ground pepper

1. Bring the vegetable stock to a boil in a medium saucepan. Stir in the quinoa and ½ teaspoon of the salt. Reduce the heat and simmer, covered, until the quinoa has absorbed all of the liquid, about 25 minutes.

2. While the quinoa is cooking, heat the olive oil in a large sauté pan over medium heat. Add the leeks and sauté until softened, about 5 minutes. Add the mushrooms and sauté until they have released their juices and reduced in size by half, about 8 minutes. Add the lemon thyme, the remaining ½ teaspoon salt, and pepper to taste.

3. Add the cooked quinoa to the leek mixture, stir to combine, and transfer to a serving bowl. Garnish with lemon thyme sprigs.

Millet with Basil Pesto, Sun-Dried Tomatoes, and Pine Nuts

Doesn't the name of this salad make your mouth water? The combination of these ingredients always makes my taste buds cheer. You can replace the pine nuts with toasted walnuts if you are looking for a more affordable option.

4 TO 6 SERVINGS

> 2 cups water
>
> 1 cup millet, rinsed
>
> ½ teaspoon sea salt
>
> ½ cup Basil Pesto (recipe follows)
>
> ½ cup oil-packed sun-dried tomatoes, thinly sliced
>
> ⅓ cup toasted pine nuts
>
> Salt and freshly ground pepper

1. Bring the water to a boil in a medium saucepan. Add the millet and salt and boil for 1 minute. Reduce the heat to low and simmer, covered, until the millet has absorbed all of the water and is fluffy, about 20 minutes.

2. Transfer the cooked millet to a large bowl and add the pesto, sun-dried tomatoes, and pine nuts. Add salt and pepper to taste.

Basil Pesto

½ CUP PESTO

> 2 cloves garlic, peeled
>
> 1½ tablespoons toasted pine nuts
>
> 1 cup basil leaves
>
> ¼ cup extra-virgin olive oil
>
> Salt and freshly ground pepper

1. Pulse the garlic in a food processor until finely chopped. Add the pine nuts and pulse just until they are ground, about 1 minute; do not let them become a paste. Add the basil and continue to pulse while slowly pouring in the olive oil. Add salt and pepper to taste.

Buckwheat Soba Noodle Salad

This is one of my favorite dishes. I adore the combination of soft, warm buckwheat noodles and intense pickled plum (umeboshi). This is a well-rounded and resplendent salad with its abundance of hues. Visit your local Asian or specialty market to find the less common ingredients used here.

4 TO 6 SERVINGS

> One 8-ounce package 100 percent buckwheat soba noodles
>
> 1½ cups broccoli florets
>
> 2 medium carrots, peeled and cut on the bias
>
> 1 cup chopped enoki mushrooms
>
> 2 tablespoons sesame oil
>
> 2 tablespoons extra-virgin olive oil
>
> 1⅔ cups cooked adzuki beans, or one 15-ounce can, drained
>
> 3 tablespoons *umeboshi* paste
>
> ½ red bell pepper, diced, for garnish
>
> 3 scallions, finely chopped, for garnish

1. Bring a pot of lightly salted water to a boil. Boil the noodles until tender, about 8 minutes.

2. While the noodles are boiling, steam the broccoli, carrots, and mushrooms in a steamer basket until slightly softened but still bright in color, about 5 minutes.

3. Strain the cooked noodles and put them in a large mixing bowl. Add the sesame oil and olive oil and toss to coat. Add the beans, steamed vegetables, and *umeboshi* paste, and thoroughly toss again, making sure the *umeboshi* paste is distributed evenly through the dish.

4. Transfer to a serving platter and garnish with diced pepper and scallions.

Chinese Green Beans

This salad was inspired by the Szechuan region of China, where salt was unavailable when its culinary traditions began. As a result, cooks there relied heavily on hot spices to flavor their foods, which made quite a delicious impression on their dishes, as evidenced by this recipe.

4 TO 6 SERVINGS

    3 tablespoons sesame oil

    2 shallots, minced

    2 cloves garlic, minced

    ½ to 1 chili pepper, seeded and minced

    1 teaspoon grated fresh gingerroot

    2 tablespoons tamari

    1 tablespoon brown rice vinegar

    2 teaspoons **maple syrup**

    1 pound green beans, trimmed

    ½ cup toasted cashews, finely chopped, for garnish

    1 tablespoon julienned Thai basil, for garnish

1. Heat the sesame oil in a large sauté pan over medium heat. Add the shallots, garlic, and chili pepper and sauté until the shallots are light brown and slightly soft, about 5 minutes. Add the gingerroot, tamari, brown rice vinegar, and maple syrup and turn off the heat.

2. While the shallot mixture is cooking, place the green beans in a steamer basket and steam until just tender and bright green, 3 to 5 minutes. As soon as the green beans have finished steaming, add them to the shallot mixture and toss to coat.

3. Transfer to a serving platter and garnish with the cashews and basil.

Balsamic-Roasted Red Garnet Yams

This dish goes well with just about anything! The sweet roasted yams contrast beautifully with the crunchy pecans and hearty greens. This dish is also a great way to get little ones to eat kale.

4 TO 6 SERVINGS

> 2 medium red garnet yams (about 2 pounds), quartered and sliced into ½-inch-thick pieces
>
> 3 shallots, finely chopped
>
> 3 tablespoons extra-virgin olive oil
>
> 2 tablespoons balsamic vinegar
>
> 1 teaspoon sea salt, divided
>
> 1 bunch kale, ribs removed, torn into bite-sized pieces
>
> ½ cup toasted pecans, finely chopped, for garnish

1. Preheat the oven to 400 degrees F.

2. In a large glass baking dish, combine the yams, shallots, olive oil, balsamic vinegar, and ½ teaspoon of the salt. Toss to coat the yams well and bake for 40 minutes on the top oven rack. Halfway through, gently turn the yams over and stir the shallots.

3. When the yams are almost done baking, steam the kale in a pot with a tight-fitting lid and a steaming basket. In a large mixing bowl, toss the steamed kale with the remaining ½ teaspoon salt. Add the yam mixture and toss well. Transfer to a serving platter and garnish with the pecans

Moroccan Bean Salad over Baby Spinach

The magical blend of saffron, ginger, turmeric, and cinnamon in this dish is so entic-ing. These velvety spiced beans atop a mountain of fresh greens create a true culinary experience.

6 SERVINGS

1 small butternut squash (about 1 pound), peeled and cubed, or 2 cups frozen diced butternut squash

1 tablespoon plus 1 teaspoon extra-virgin olive oil

1 medium yellow onion, quartered and thinly sliced

½ teaspoon ground turmeric

½ teaspoon ground ginger

¼ teaspoon ground cinnamon

¼ teaspoon saffron threads

1 yellow bell pepper, diced

1 cup cooked or canned large lima beans or fava beans

1¼ teaspoons sea salt, divided

6 cups loosely packed baby spinach

3 tablespoons white balsamic vinegar

1 medium Pink Lady apple, thinly sliced

⅔ cup toasted slivered almonds

Freshly ground black pepper

1. Steam the squash in a pot with a tight-fitting lid and steamer basket until tender, 15 to 20 minutes. Set aside.

2. Heat the olive oil in a sauté pan over medium heat. Add the onion and sauté until slightly soft, about 5 minutes. Add the turmeric, ginger, cinnamon, and saffron, and stir to coat the onion. Cook, stirring, until the onions are translucent, about 5 min-utes. Add the bell pepper and cook for another 5 minutes. Reduce the heat to low, add the beans, 1 teaspoon of the salt, and the reserved squash, and remove the pan from the heat.

3. Divide the spinach among 6 salad plates. Drizzle with the remaining olive oil, white balsamic vinegar, and salt. Divide the squash mixture evenly among the plates in the center of the spinach. Top with the apples, almonds, and pepper to taste.

Asian Kale

Nothing feels more wholesome than munching down on a big plateful of this colorful salad. The crisp, bright green leaves, interspersed with orange carrots and red pepper, are guaranteed to make you feel good. The sprinkling of gomasio—*a traditional Asian sesame salt—really gives this salad a unique and healthy flavor.*

4 TO 6 SERVINGS

> 1 bunch kale, ribs removed, thinly sliced
>
> 2 small carrots, peeled and julienned
>
> 1 red bell pepper, diced
>
> 2 tablespoons *gomasio*

Dressing

> 3 cloves garlic, minced
>
> 1 teaspoon grated fresh gingerroot
>
> 1½ tablespoons sesame oil
>
> 2 tablespoons extra-virgin olive oil
>
> 2 tablespoons tamari
>
> 1¾ tablespoons brown rice vinegar
>
> ¼ cup toasted pumpkin seeds

1. Combine the kale, carrots, and bell pepper in a large bowl.

2. Prepare the dressing. In a small bowl, combine the garlic, gingerroot, sesame oil, olive oil, tamari, and brown rice vinegar. Mix well.

3. Pour the dressing over the kale mixture and marinate for at least 30 minutes—the longer the salad marinates, the stronger the flavors will be. Toss with pumpkin seeds and *gomasio* before serving.

Hijiki Carrot Slaw

This spectacular salad is incredibly healthy for you; it is full of the fiber and minerals that your body needs. Make it with the Chinese Green Beans (page 153) and Buckwheat Soba Noodle Salad (page 152) for a wonderful Asian-inspired meal.

6 SERVINGS

> One 2.1-ounce package *hijiki*, rinsed and soaked in water for 10 minutes
>
> ¾ pound carrots (about 7 small carrots), peeled and grated
>
> 3 tablespoons toasted sesame oil
>
> 3 tablespoons brown rice vinegar
>
> 1½ tablespoons tamari
>
> 1 avocado, peeled and chopped
>
> 2½ tablespoons *gomasio*, divided
>
> 1 medium tomato, seeded and sliced, for garnish (optional)

1. In a large bowl, combine the *hijiki*, carrots, sesame oil, brown rice vinegar, and tamari, and toss to combine. Add the avocado and 2 tablespoons of the *gomasio* and lightly toss.

2. Transfer to a serving platter and garnish with the remaining ½ tablespoon *gomasio* and the tomato.

Cherry Tomatoes with Fresh Herbs and White Balsamic Vinegar

This is a simple, fresh, and zesty salad that will never go to waste. Make this ahead of time, giving the herbs a chance to release their full flavors.

4 TO 6 SERVINGS

1 pint cherry tomatoes, halved

½ cup finely julienned fresh basil

1 tablespoon chopped fresh lemon thyme

¼ cup finely snipped fresh chives

½ medium red onion, finely diced

1 tablespoon white balsamic vinegar

½ teaspoon sea salt

1½ tablespoons extra-virgin olive oil, divided

4 cups mixed baby greens

Freshly ground black pepper

1. In a large bowl, combine the tomatoes, basil, lemon thyme, chives, onion, white balsamic vinegar, salt, and 1 tablespoon of the olive oil. Marinate at room temperature for 30 minutes.

2. In a large bowl, toss the baby greens with the remaining ½ tablespoon olive oil. Divide the greens among individual salad plates, top with the tomato mixture, and season to taste with pepper.

Sweet Golden Beets with Toasted Pecans and Currants

A very talented woman named Heather Curtis, who has been a great leader at the Flying Apron, created this recipe. What a gorgeous contribution this salad is!

6 TO 8 SERVINGS

> 3 tablespoons water
>
> 2 tablespoons **maple syrup**
>
> 3 medium golden beets (about 1 pound), peeled, halved, and julienned
>
> 2 bunches regular or dinosaur kale, ribs removed, chopped into bite-sized pieces
>
> ⅓ cup dried currants
>
> ½ cup chopped toasted pecans

Dressing

> ⅓ cup balsamic vinegar
>
> 1 cup extra-virgin olive oil
>
> ¼ teaspoon freshly ground pepper
>
> ½ teaspoon freshly squeezed lemon juice
>
> ¼ teaspoon Dijon mustard
>
> 2 tablespoons **maple syrup**

1. In a saucepan, bring the water and maple syrup to a boil. Place the beets in a steamer basket and steam until they are fork-tender, about 10 minutes. Strain and transfer to a large bowl. Add the kale, currants, and pecans.

2. In a small bowl, combine the balsamic vinegar, olive oil, pepper, lemon juice, Dijon mustard, and maple syrup. Whisk thoroughly.

3. Pour the dressing over the beet mixture and toss to combine.

Pea Shoot, Chive, and Apricot Salad with Honey Mustard Dressing

I first served this salad at a company party, and it earned such rave reviews that we started serving it regularly at the bakery. The seasonal flavors of the pea shoots and apricots, combined with the light honey mustard dressing, make a salad you'll look forward to serving to your friends and family.

4 TO 6 SERVINGS

4 cups loosely packed pea shoots

4 cups mixed baby greens

6 scallions or chives, cut on the bias into 1-inch pieces

½ cup sugar snap peas, cut on the bias into 1-inch pieces

½ cup snow peas, halved

5 fresh apricots, cut into thin wedges, for garnish

Dressing

3 tablespoons white balsamic vinegar

½ tablespoon **honey** or **maple syrup**

1 clove garlic, minced

1 tablespoon Dijon mustard

Sea salt and freshly ground pepper

½ cup extra-virgin olive oil

1. In a large bowl, combine the pea shoots, baby greens, scallions, sugar snap peas, and snow peas.

2. Prepare the dressing. In a small bowl, combine the white balsamic vinegar, honey, garlic, Dijon mustard, and salt and pepper to taste. Whisk thoroughly. While continuing to whisk, add the olive oil in a steady stream.

3. Pour the dressing over the salad and toss to combine. Garnish with the apricots.

Dinosaur Kale, Artichoke, and Garbanzo Bean Salad

This is a great salad to make ahead and have on hand for packed lunches and snacks. The strong leaves of the kale hold up well, even overnight.

4 TO 6 SERVINGS

> 1 bunch dinosaur kale, ribs removed, torn into bite-sized pieces
>
> 3 tablespoons extra-virgin olive oil
>
> Juice of ½ lemon
>
> 1 teaspoon sea salt
>
> One 6-ounce jar artichoke hearts, drained and quartered
>
> 1⅔ cups cooked garbanzo beans, or one 15-ounce can, drained
>
> 3 medium tomatoes, chopped

1. In a large bowl, combine the kale, olive oil, lemon juice, and salt. Massage the dressing into the kale with your hands. Add the artichoke hearts, garbanzo beans, and tomatoes. Toss to combine.

Resources

Aunt Patty's Natural Foods & Ingredients
www.auntpattys.com
For canola oil, molasses, brown rice syrup, nuts, seeds, and agave syrup

Bob's Red Mill
5000 SE International Way
Milwaukie, OR 97222
800-349-2173
www.bobsredmill.com
For garbanzo bean flour, fava bean flour, brown rice flour, yeast, xanthan gum, and many other gluten-free products

Dagoba Organic Chocolate
2000 Folsom Street
San Francisco, CA 94110
866-237-0152
www.dagobachocolate.com
For dairy-free dark chocolate chips

Florida Crystals Corporation
1 N Clematis Street, Suite 200
West Palm Beach, FL 33401
877-835-2828
www.floridacrystals.com
For organic whole cane sugar

GloryBee Foods
P.O. Box 2744
Eugene, OR 97402
800-456-7923
www.glorybee.com
For oils, sweeteners, honey, nuts, seeds, and nut butters

Lundberg Family Farms
P.O. Box 369
Richvale, CA 95974
530-882-4551
www.lundberg.com
For brown rice flour, brown rice syrup, and rice milk

Mystic Lake Dairy
24200 NE 14th Street
Sammamish, WA 98074
206-868-2029
For concentrated fruit juice

Quinoa Corporation
310-217-8125
www.quinoa.net
For quinoa flour

RED STAR Yeast
P.O. Box 737
Milwaukee, WI 53201
877-677-7000
www.redstaryeast.com
For cake and active dry yeast

Spectrum Naturals
4600 Sleepytime Drive
Boulder, CO 80301
800-434-4246
www.spectrumorganics.com
For palm oil and coconut oil

Acknowledgments

I would like to thank my family—William Dowd, Kathy Gordon, Elizabeth Dowd, Malcolm Edwards, and Julie and Andrew Fern—for their constant enthusiasm, support, and love. Thank you, Dad, especially, for the strength, wisdom, sense of humor, and immense energy that you have given to the bakery all these years. I would also like to thank Jerrolynn Katzinger for providing me with the first edit of the cookbook—I can see why her students are such great readers! And thanks to both Leon and Jer for being such strong, loving forces in our lives. I am especially grateful to my husband, Joseph, who always gives me confidence to follow my dreams and sustains my energy with his encouragement and unyielding love. A great many thanks to Jessica Sanborn for her descriptive insights, zest for the bakery, and powerful friendship. I am grateful to Benjamin L'Esperance and Heather Curtis for giving so much of themselves to running the Flying Apron Bakery, which has allowed me the time to write this cookbook. A very special thanks to the Flying Apron team, who continually amaze me with their dedication. A tremendous thanks to the talented team at Sasquatch Books who have made this such a beautiful cookbook. Many thanks to Terence Maikels; it is because of his prompting, keenness, and zeal that this book came to be.

INDEX

About the Author

Photo by Rachelle Longé

Jennifer Katzinger is the owner and co-founder of the Flying Apron Bakery in Seattle. Flying Apron opened its doors seven years ago and has become a local favorite, widely known for its unique niche offerings. Flying Apron is a gluten-free, dairy-free, egg-free, and soy-free bakery/café that uses many alternative sweeteners, unrefined flours, and organic ingredients.

Jennifer earned a BA in English Literature from the University of Washington and from there went on to pursue a Master's in Industrial Design from the Pratt Institute in New York. She has been creating in the kitchen since she was knee-high. Her love of inventing recipes with lesser-known ingredients in the pursuit of delight and sustainability is what continues to drive her. She introduces this cookbook at a time when more and more people are finding it necessary to change their culinary habits and strive for greater health.

As Washington natives, Jennifer and her husband, Joseph, and their dog, Neve, are avid hikers of the surrounding Cascade and Olympic mountains. Jennifer and Joseph are recent first-time parents and happily look forward to sharing their traditions and love of delicious and wholesome meals with their daughter, Lillian.